The Low Fat Diet
Special Diet Cookbook

100 delicious ways to cut right down on fat

The Low Fat Diet

Special Diet Cookbook

Sarah Bounds

Thorsons
An Imprint of HarperCollinsPublishers

Thorsons
An Imprint of HarperCollins*Publishers*
77-85 Fulham Palace Road,
Hammersmith, London W6 8JB

First published as *Fat-Free Cooking* 1985
This revised edition published by Thorsons 1991
1 3 5 7 9 10 8 6 4 2

A catalogue record for this book
is available from the British Library

ISBN 0 7225 1173 6

Typeset by Harper Phototypesetters Limited,
Northampton, England
Printed in Great Britain by
The Bath Press, Bath, Avon

Contents

Introduction

Heart disease is the biggest single cause of death in the West today. We suffer from one of the worst rates of heart disease in the world. Isn't it time we all made the effort to consider why we're more likely to die of heart disease than any other illness?

Doctors and scientific researchers are united in their belief that one of the most positive steps that each of us can take in helping to cut the incidence of heart disease is to reduce the fat content of our diet. Couple this with stopping smoking, losing weight, controlling blood pressure and taking up regular exercise and each of us could make our future prospects a lot rosier.

Cutting down on fat also reaps other rewards.

Fat is the richest source of calories in food, so cutting down the amount of fat we eat will help us control weight problems — and since 40 per cent of us are overweight, that's no bad thing either. A diet that is lower in fat doesn't mean a life of denial; there are plenty of foods that are naturally low in fat that can be eaten in abundance. Rather, it's a case of taking more care over the choice of foods we buy and the way we cook and serve them.

This book is full of practical advice on choosing and using foods to help us cut down on fat and in so doing ensure that we enjoy a better quality of health, today and tomorrow.

Chapter 1

What is Fat?

Fat fuels the body. The energy expenditure involved in day-to-day living requires fuel from the food we eat. This it obtains, via complex pathways, from carbohydrates and from fats. We tend to think of butter, lard or margarine when we think of fat, but fat is found in many varied foods and although almost a quarter of the fat in the typical Western diet comes from butter and margarine, the second biggest proportion comes from meats, with milk following close behind.

Reducing the amount of fat in the diet is not just a simple matter of being mean with the margarine on your bread. It also involves cutting down on other foods like meat, eggs, cheese, milk, cakes, pastries and biscuits (cookies) — foods where the fat is hidden. We eat more hidden fat than we do visible fat so achieving a diet that is low in fat involves reviewing *all* the foods eaten, rather than just the fat we put on our food on the plate.

Whether hidden in cakes or meat or coming from a bottle of oil or a margarine tub, all fat is chemically similar. Fats belong to a complex group of substances called lipids. Lipids are found in many places in nature, not least in our own bodies. The fats we eat in food however are known as triglycerides, made up of glycerol and fatty acids. While glycerol always remains constant, fatty acids can vary and the specific fatty acid found in a particular fat will influence how it tastes, smells and appears to us. Most triglycerides mix different fatty acids together — each molecule consists of one part glycerol and three parts fatty acids, hence the name *tri*glyceride.

Explaining Fatty Acids

There are over 40 different fatty acids found in nature. Although they are chemically similar, there are differences in their structure and it is these differences that underline the different forms of fats that we eat. These fatty acids fall into three distinct chemical groups, depending on their formula:

- saturated
- unsaturated, or, mono-unsaturated
- polyunsaturated

This method of classifying fatty acids reflects the degree of saturation of a fatty acid. Saturation is a term used to describe the chemical structure of a fatty acid. If there is one double bond in the formula, the fatty acid is said to be unsaturated, or, mono-unsaturated. More than one double bond in the formula means that it is poly-unsaturated, and where no double bonds are present, the fatty acid is said to be saturated.

A fat consisting mainly of saturated fatty acids will tend to be solid at room temperature. A fat containing a large proportion of unsaturated or polyunsaturated fatty acids, will be likely to be liquid at room temperature. Fats liquid at room temperature are said to be oils but, as we shall see, oils are not always as unsaturated as they appear. Conversely, not all firm fats are as saturated as others.

It is worth understanding the chemical shorthand used to describe fatty acids as this reveals the degree of saturation. Here are a few examples of some of the more common fatty acids.

- Saturated fatty acids
butyric acid	C4:0
palmitic acid	C16:0
stearic acid	C18:0

- Unsaturated fatty acids
oleic acid	C18:1
erucic acid	C22:1

- Polyunsaturated fatty acids
linoleic acid	C18:2
linolenic acid	C18:3
arachidonic acid	C20:4

The 'C' represents carbon atoms, the first number indicating the number of carbon atoms present in the formula of the fatty acid. The last digit shows the number of double bonds. Hence, linoleic acid has 18 carbon atoms and 2 double bonds, whereas linolenic acid has 18 carbon atoms and 3 double bonds.

It is particularly important to understand these two fatty acids because they are required by the body to perform vital functions and cannot be synthesized by the body. They are therefore called the essential fatty acids. Both linoleic and linolenic acids are polyunsaturated but they belong to two different fat families. Linolenic acid — or, more correctly, alpha-linolenic acid — (LNA) — belongs to the Omega 3 fatty acid family; linoleic acid (LA) belongs to the Omega 6 fatty acid family. In the body these two fatty acids are converted by a series of complex chemical steps into substances called prosta-glandins (PGEs), which in turn perform a whole range of different functions.

PGEs help to control the body's immune system, healing and repair processes, digestion and reproduction, brain function and the workings of the heart and cardiovascular system — the list of jobs performed by PGEs is varied and impressive and the two Omega 3 and Omega 6 families of fatty acids are each converted into a separate group of PGEs essential for health.

Recent research on fats in the body has

centred on the role of the two Omega types of fat and the specific functions performed by the prostaglandins they produce. Few people will not have heard of fish oils or evening primrose oil. In recent years researchers have identified how these oils are broken down in the body and the subsequent influence they can have on health. Take the fish oils. Oils from oil-rich fish such as herring, mackerel, salmon and trout are Omega 3 fats. Two fatty acids, EPA and DHA, are found in particularly high concentrations in these oils and these two fatty acids are involved in the breakdown of LNA to the vital PGE3 series of prostaglandins in the body. Specific functions of this group, which have particular relevance in heart disease, include keeping the blood less sticky and less likely to clot. Evening primrose oil on the other hand is involved specifically in the breakdown of Omega 6 fats in the body. The oil is the richest natural source of GLA — gamma-linolenic acid — which is produced in the body when linolenic acid is converted into the prostaglandins. Research has revealed that in some people the body's ability to break down linolenic acid to GLA (and hence to the prostaglandins) is blocked. In such cases, taking a supplement of evening primrose oil supplies a ready-made source of GLA and is now believed to be capable of helping to treat a varied number of symptoms, such as eczema, PMS, breast disease and hyperactivity.

Technical though these discussions are, one thing is clear — fats are vital to health maintenance. However, the exact role a fat will play will depend on its own chemistry. The recent work on the Omega 3 and Omega 6 fats and the prostaglandins they produce has provided more detailed knowledge of fats' potential in helping to control many problems of ill health. This said, for most people the heart of the fat issue is still the same as it was ten years ago — saturated versus polyunsaturated fat and the role of cholesterol in heart disease. Every now and then a new study is published that might show one or other in a bad light, only to be contradicted, apparently, by the *next* study's results. The issue is probably the most hotly contested in the nutrition world and the picture is usually further confused by vested interests. There are, however, some basic facts. We know that most people in the West eat too much fat. We know therefore that most people should cut down on their fat consumption. We know that polyunsaturated fatty acids play vital roles in health maintenance. These basic facts form the basis of sensible nutritional advice for everyone: cut down on fat, reducing in particular the amount of saturated fat in your diet.

The cholesterol question

Eating too much fat will raise the level of cholesterol in the blood, particularly if that fat is saturated fat. Saturated fat, which tends to come from animal foods such as red meats and dairy produce, encourages the body to make more cholesterol than it needs or can get rid of. To complicate matters there are two types of cholesterol involved: the 'good' cholesterol, known as high density lipoproteins (HDL), and the 'bad' cholesterol, low density lipoprotein (LDL).

When we eat, the LDLs carry the fat in the blood to the cells of the body where it is required to fuel various activities. What's left that is surplus to requirements should be taken to the liver and subsequently excreted from the body, but if there is too much LDL in the blood or if there is a basic malfunction in the system, some of that fat will, instead, become deposited on the walls of the arteries as plaque. Plaque deposits gradually build up over the years when excessive amounts of fat are eaten and the arteries gradually become narrowed, which means that the heart has to work much harder to pump blood round the system. Silting up of the arteries is one of the most common causes of heart attacks and strokes and the process can begin in childhood when a fat-rich diet is eaten. In contrast to the silting up with LDLs, the good HDLs actually help to boost the transport of fat to the liver for subsequent removal. They act as efficient cleaners of the system, helping to clear out the debris and keep things working smoothly. The higher the level of HDL in ratio to the total level of fat in the blood the better.

How do you know if the fat you are eating will play a positive or negative role in the body? The answer is not clear-cut, but essentially the saturated fats will increase the body's production of LDLs whereas polyunsaturated fats generally do not. While polyunsaturated fats do perform vital functions in the body, a high consumption can lead to other problems. Potentially damaging substances called free radicals can be formed when an excessive intake of polyunsaturated fats is consumed and is not protected by substances called antioxidants. Antioxidants, which include vitamins C, E and the minerals zinc and selenium, help to protect the fragile fatty acids

from free radical formation. So while it can be helpful to increase the level of polyunsaturated fats in the diet, it is clear that it must be at the expense of saturated fat and it must coincide with an overall reduction in the total amount of fat we are eating.

Another important aspect of polyunsaturated fats is their vulnerability to breakdown by the formation of 'trans' fats that block any beneficial effect that fat might have. As well as preventing the work of the essential fatty acids, trans fats also behave more like saturated fats in the body, raising the level of LDLs. Trans fats tend to be formed during food processing, especially during the hydrogenation of fats in the hardening of margarine manufacture, but few food companies actually declare their presence.

Finally, a word on the third group of fatty acids — the unsaturated, or, mono-unsaturated fatty acids. These are often found naturally in fats and oils and are generally thought to have a neutral effect on the body — that is they don't do the harm of saturated fats but neither do they play a positive role in health maintenance. Olive oil is rich in these unsaturated fatty acids and this is one reason for the recent resurgence in its popularity.

Heart Healthy Factors

If you're worried about your chances of developing heart disease, the first step to take is to have a cholesterol check to show how high the level of total cholesterol is in your blood. The most reliable tests will also show the level of the beneficial HDL in the blood. Generally a figure of 5.2mmol cholesterol per litre is desirable — ideally the level should be at or lower than this. A ratio of 3:1 total cholesterol to HDL would indicate an average risk of heart disease — the higher the level of HDL in relation to the total the better. Blood cholesterol, however, important as it is as an indicator of the state of health of your heart, is not the only means by which we can assess our chances of developing heart disease. There are a number of risk factors, of which a high level of blood fats is but one. The more risk factors you have, the greater your chance of developing heart problems. It makes sense to act positively and eliminate or reduce as many of these risks as possible. They include:

- **smoking** a cigarette smoker is twice as likely to have a heart attack as a non-smoker, so give it up

- **high blood pressure** a healthy heart is helped by a good level of blood pressure — have yours checked regularly by your doctor who will advise you on the ideal level

- **being overweight** overweight people put an unnecessary burden on their body so those with a weight problem very often have high blood pressure and a high cholesterol level, too

- **alcohol** a little alcohol seems to help to raise the level of HDLs in the blood, but too much and the effect is stopped and blood pressure is raised

- **family history** heart disease often runs in families and, although there is nothing you can do to change the past, you can help to make your future healthier by eliminating as many of the other risk factors as possible

- **exercise** maximize your health by taking regular exercise, ideally two or three times a week, sustained to raise your pulse rate for 15-20 minutes at a time — try jogging, swimming, cycling or simply walking briskly.

In addition to the above, try some of the things listed below:

- **taking garlic** there is now considerable scientific evidence that taking a regular garlic oil supplement can help to lower cholesterol levels and, because garlic possesses anti-clogging properties, it can generally help assist the flow of blood in the arteries (in Germany the research has led to garlic being a licensed preventive medicine for heart and circulatory diseases)

- **managing stress** learning to relax and to control the level of stress in your life can help to lessen the chance of blood pressure rising

- **eating well** as well as cutting down on fat and eating the right type of fat, ensuring that there are plenty of vital vitamins and minerals present in the food you eat will ensure that the many varied functions performed by these substances can be carried out to the full, so choose fresh, nutritious foods, including plenty of fresh fruit and vegetables every day.

Why Less is Better

Fat is the most concentrated source of calories in the diet. One tiny gram of fat will supply the body with 9 calories, so 100 grams, roughly 4 ounces, of pure fat will contain a hefty 900 calories — almost half a woman's daily requirement.

In practice we don't eat much pure fat. Fat in our diet comes from the visible fats we spread and cook with and from the hidden fats in meat, cheese, pastries, ice-cream and so on. Our love of fatty, rich foods contributes directly to two of the West's most common health problems — being overweight and heart disease.

Cutting down on the amount of fat we eat means an immediate cut in calories consumed and, as we have seen, cutting down on fat in total and paying attention to the *type* of fat consumed can help to boost the health of the heart. There's evidence, too, that certain forms of cancer might be related at least in part to a high-fat diet. In addition, cutting down on fat might help relieve rheumatoid arthritis and multiple sclerosis. Generally, though, anyone can benefit from eating a diet that is lower in fat. Making the effort to choose foods that are naturally lower in fat and cooking by methods that add only the minimum of extra fat will mean using healthier foods as the basis of eating. Foods that have undergone little processing retain more of the natural vitamins and minerals and plant foods, such as cereals, will, in addition, have a higher level of vital dietary fibre. As well as cutting down on fat, most people today could benefit from switching to a style of eating that is also higher in fibre and higher in vital vitamins and minerals while containing less sugar. It's the best all round recipe for a healther way of eating and living.

Chapter 2

Planning a Low-fat Diet

There are two basic rules for eating a low-fat diet:

1 choose foods low in fat, especially those low in saturated fat

2 avoid or restrict the amount of extra fat added during cooking and serving.

The general consensus of opinion is that the amount of energy (or calories) supplied by fat should be reduced to 30 per cent of the total — the rest coming from carbohydrates like starch and sugar and from protein. For an average calorie intake of 2,200 a day that equates to 2½ oz (73g) fat — that's not a lot!

Choosing Foods Low in Fat

Much of the fat in the food we eat is hidden fat, so cutting down on fat means watching carefully for foods that might contain invisible fat. Meat, for example, is commonly eaten in the mistaken belief that if visible fat around the outside of a joint (cut) or steak is trimmed away, the rest will be free of fat. This is not so, as all lean meat contains a certain amount of fat. The red meats — lamb, pork and beef — are high in saturated fats and so are the products made from them. Meat products account for almost one-tenth of the fat in the typical diet, while meats themselves account for around 18 per cent. Cutting down on meat and on the amount of meat products like sausages, meat pies and cold meats, will make a big difference to your fat intake.

If red meats are to be restricted or cut out of the diet then something is needed to replace them. Many find that poultry fills this gap well. Chicken and turkey are not only low in fat, but contain some polyunsaturated fatty acids, too. Game is another low-fat food, but duck, for example, can be fatty if the skin is eaten (this goes for poultry, too, so always remove the skin before cooking or eating).

Fish is becoming increasingly popular once again and while many people are beginning to reject meat and poultry on ethical grounds, fish living free in the oceans is a more acceptable and healthier alternative. Fish is classified into two groups, oily and white. If you think that perhaps oily fish should be excluded from a low-fat diet, then think again! Oily fish like mackerel and herrings, as we have seen, contain particular types of polyunsaturated fatty acids (known as EPA and DHA) that help to keep the blood thin and less prone to unwanted clotting. Regular amounts of these fish should be eaten as well as the less fatty white fish like cod, plaice (flounder) and haddock. White fish, however, is traditionally drowned in fat when cooked, so care needs to be taken in choosing methods of cooking that will not add large amounts of fat.

Dairy products are another undesirable fatty food. Most of the fat found in milk, eggs and cheese, is highly saturated and should be restricted. This does not mean suddenly banning all dairy foods, rather, it entails choosing dairy foods carefully.

Milk

Full-fat milk contains nearly 4 per cent fat, but the fat in milk can be easily removed in the dairy by skimming. The resultant milk will contain only 0.1 per cent fat and half the calories of the original products. Fresh and long life skimmed milk is now easy to buy and dried skimmed milk powders are available, too, but make sure they do not contain added vegetable fats. Semi-skimmed milk is also available, but this will only have had some of the fat removed, and this too is available both fresh and in long-life cartons.

Cheese

Hard cheese is one third fat, while Continental cheeses such as Camembert and Edam contain only 23 and 20 per cent respectively. Not surprisingly it is hard to justify eating much cheese in a diet that is desirably low in fat. Few of the recipes in this book contain cheese, but if they do then the cheese is used in a small quantity as a topping and is one of the new 'breeds' of cheese now available made to resemble, say, Cheddar cheese while containing only 15 per cent fat, compared to the standard 33 per cent fat usually found in this type of cheese. There are also low-fat versions of soft cheese, such as smooth white cream cheese or cottage (pot) cheese, and these contain considerably less fat than their conventional counterparts. Look out, too, for cheeses sold as quark or curd (cottage) cheese as they also have lower fat contents. Wherever the word 'skimmed' is used this implies less fat is present, but subtle variations exist as products may be called 'low-fat' or 'reduced fat'. The same confusion exists with yogurt, too, as yogurt may be made from skimmed milk or, at the other extreme, from full-fat milk. Look carefully at the label. Clearer labelling, such as that in America, is definitely required so that the fat content of foods can be easily established on the shelf.

Eggs

Eggs have gained rather a bad reputation in recent years because of the cholesterol they contain. It is true that eggs supply saturated fat and cholesterol, but they should not be eliminated from the diet completely because they are valuable sources of iron and of B vitamins. Try to limit their consumption and to use them in cooking where a little can be shared between a few people, rather than serving up a dish of scrambled eggs to each person. Free-range eggs are preferable because they have been produced by more humane methods.

Just as eggs should not be completely avoided, because of other nutrients they contain, so milk and cheese are important source of calcium and of vitamins A and D. However some people are allergic to milk and others find that its tendency to form mucus in the body affects their sinuses and so they choose to avoid dairy foods.

Fibre

Like meat, fish and poultry, dairy foods are devoid of fibre. Much interest is now being paid to dietary fibre, once called roughage. The NACNE report calls for an increase in the amount of fibre in the diet from the present average of ¾ oz (20g) a day to 1 oz (30g). Animal foods do not supply any fibre; it is up to the plant foods we eat to provide us with this vital ingredient.

Fibre is essential for a healthy digestive system, to keep the contents of the intestines flowing freely so guarding against constipation. It is now thought that a good fibre intake and the avoidance of constipation may well reduce the risks of other more threatening diseases such as diverticulitis, appendicitis, hernia and bowel cancer. In the past few years attention has switched to the potential role of fibre in helping prevent heart disease. This is because there are two types of fibre — insoluble fibre, of which wheat bran is the richest source, and soluble fibre, of which oat and rice bran are the richest sources. Existing work on fibre centred on the role of the insoluble fibres, but more recently there has been evidence that soluble fibre possesses the ability to lower blood cholesterol levels. Manufacturers have responded by launching a whole range of oat bran-based breakfast cereals. Although there is still a certain amount of confusion over the medical trials that were performed, increasing the amount of oats in your diet certainly won't do you any harm and may well do some positive good. Fibre, both soluble and insoluble, is found in grains, pulses (legumes), nuts, seeds, fruits and vegetables and these ingredients are also useful for their comparatively low fat content. Fruits and vegetables are valuable for the level of vitamin C, minerals and other vitamins they contain and they also contribute to the fibre intake of the diet. More significant though are the grains, pulses (legumes), nuts and seeds because as well as supplying fibre in good quantities, they also supply protein. In diets where meat intake is being reduced it is important to make the most of the plant protein foods. These fall into three distinct groups:

- **grains** wheat, rice, rye, barley, oats, millet, buckwheat
- **pulses (legumes)** peas, beans and lentils
- **nuts and seeds** walnuts (English walnuts), almonds, Brazils, cashews, etc., and sesame and sunflower seeds.

In the West, wheat is our most important plant protein and for maximum nutritive value it should be eaten in the whole grain form or as wholemeal (whole wheat) flour where the nutrients present in the original wheat grain are preserved virtually intact. Refining wheat to produce white flour removes much of the fibre, vitamins and minerals. The same applies to other cereals, too, so always choose products like brown rice, unpolished pearl (pot) barley, wholemeal (whole wheat) pasta and wholemeal (whole wheat) flour for cooking. Grains contain only small amounts of fat and so are valuable in supply the vital protein our bodies need for growth and repair processes, without the large amounts of fat that meat and dairy foods tend to supply.

Peas, beans and lentils are, similarly, good choices for a low fat diet. Their low level of fat, combined with their high fibre and protein levels, make them important ingredients. There are so many different types of pulses (legumes) that they are a versatile food. Lentils, different beans, dried peas can be used in many savoury dishes to take the place of meat or, if preferred, to 'extend' the meat so that less is eaten per portion.

Nuts and seeds are another important source of plant protein and contain fibre, but they are higher in fat than grains or pulses (legumes). However the fat is less saturated than that found in animal foods, and their rich flavour make them a valuable ingredient in composite dishes such as nut burgers and loaves.

When using plant protein foods a simple combining rule should be followed to ensure that the most is made of the protein contained within the foods. Two of the three different groups should be eaten together to balance each other out — so mix grains with pulses (legumes) or nuts at a meal or mix nuts with pulses (legumes).

Alternatively, balance the protein in, say, grains with a dairy food, fish, poultry or meat. In other words mix either a plant food with an animal food or mix two plant protein foods together at a meal. It is usually instinctive to mix ingredients together anyway to provide interesting meals.

Sweet foods often contain a surprisingly high proportion of fat and so it is preferable to keep desserts simple and to avoid processed cakes, biscuits (cookies) and pastries. Concentrate instead of making the most of both fresh and dried fruits. Avoid chocolate and sweets — not only for their fat but also for their high sugar content.

Fats on the Table

Spreading and cooking with fats and oils obviously adds calories and raises the overall fat content of the diet quite dramatically. In practice it is both difficult and relatively unpalatable to cut out *all* 'extra' fat, so it then becomes important to choose more carefully what fat you add, remembering, of course, that whatever spread or oil you choose it must be used sparingly.

Oils

Oils high in polyunsaturated fatty acids (PUFA) tend to be less stable to heat than olive oil, which is high in the unsaturated fatty acids. Cooking with a small amount of olive oil is probably the best option, reserving the PUFA-rich oils, like safflower, sunflower and corn, for salad dressings, which do not entail heating the oil.

Spreads

Many people mistakenly believe that *all* margarines are 'better' than butter. This is both untrue and misleading. Many margarines, especially the hard or block margarines, contain just as much saturated fat as butter. The best choice is a product that is specifically labelled as high in PUFA and these are usually made from sunflower or soya oils. Look at the label for the exact breakdown of fatty acids and avoid any declaring high levels of the trans fats. In recent years the nutritional labelling of food has improved considerably. With big retailers lead-ing the way, it is now possible to see the exact levels of fat on many products — not just on margarines and spreads. In the past few years there has been an increase, too, in the number of low-fat and very-low-fat spreads available. These have the advantage of containing higher levels of non-fat substances and hence lower levels of fats, but they are so highly processed that they tend to contain large numbers of additives, too. They could prove useful, however, in some situations, but generally it is wiser to try to learn once and for all to cut down on visible fats like these in the diet.

Table 1: *Fatty Acids in Food Fats*

Product	Saturated %	Unsaturated %	PUFA %
Coconut oil	75.9	7.0	1.8
Corn oil	17.2	30.7	51.6
Olive oil	14.7	73.0	11.7
Palm oil	47.4	43.6	8.7
Peanut or groundnut oil	19.7	50.1	29.8
Safflower oil	10.7	13.2	75.5
Sunflower oil	13.7	33.3	52.3
Beef dripping	43.1	48.3	4.3
Lard	44.0	44.0	9.5

Table 2: *The Fatty Acid Contents of Commercial Spreads*
(Figures for supermarket own-label products have not been included)

Product	Total fat in g	S	M	P
Vitalite	80	15	24	41
Vitalite Light	59	10	18	29
St Ivel Gold	36.8	10	19	6
St Ivel Gold Lowest	25	6.5	13.5	3.5

Product	Total fat in g	S	M	P
Shape	36.8	8.7	10.4	16
Flora	80	14	na	40
Baking Flora	82	19	na	38
Blue Band	82	18	na	38
Stork SB	81	23-30	na	8-15
Stork (block)	81	25-35	na	2-10
Echo	81	25-35	na	2-10
Krona	70	29	na	8
Stork Light Blend	60	17-22	na	6-11
Olivio	60	11	na	13
Flora Extra Light	39	7	na	19
Delight	39.8	12	na	7
Delight Extra Low	20	4	na	6
Outline	25	5	na	7

S = saturated in g
M = mono-unsaturated in g
P = PUFA in g
na = figures not available from manufacturers

Avoid Adding Fat

Having chosen the right ingredients, make sure you add only the minimum of fat during cooking and serving.

Avoid:

- roasting
- frying
- sautéing

as these methods all add extra fat. Choose instead methods like:

- poaching
- grilling (broiling)
- steaming
- braising
- baking

as these are all successful without added fat.

Take potatoes as an example. Raw potatoes contain 0.1 per cent fat; mashed with margarine and milk they contain 5 per cent fat; roasted potatoes contain 4.8 per cent and converted into chips (fries) they contain 10.9 per cent fat. If they are boiled or baked in their jackets then the figure remains at 0.1 per cent fat — that is until eaters smother them with butter at the table!

The secret of low-fat cooking is to keep added fat to a minimum and to compensate for any flavour loss by making dishes more interesting with the addition of herbs, spices or well-flavoured stocks. This will also help you to cut down on the amount of salt added to food, which may help to control blood pressure.

Several of the recipes in this book require ingredients to be sautéed. If liked, a little well-flavoured vegetable stock can be used in place of fat, or a small amount of a vegetable oil that is high in polyunsaturated fatty acids (see Table 1, page 19) can be used. As noted earlier, the body needs polyunsaturated fatty acids, particularly linoleic and linolenic acid as these are essential to health, so a small amount of oil *is* necessary. These fatty acids are also found in small amounts in plant protein foods such as nuts, seeds and grains.

Often fat is used to make pies, pastries and other baked goods. Try to restrict the amount of pastry in the diet — after all, shortcrust pastry is about one-third fat, and richer pastries contain even more. Reserve such dishes for occasional special treats; the same is true of cakes and biscuits (cookies). Chapter 7 contains some recipes for baking that are lower in fat than most conventional recipes.

Entertaining guests usually involves the use of fat-rich foods as these tend to be linked in our mind with luxury. However, if you enjoy entertaining and tend to do so rather a lot, start to ring the changes and serve low-fat dishes to your guests. They will benefit as well as yourself! You'll find plenty of special recipes in Chapter 8 for various formal and informal occasions.

Table 3: *Did You Know . . .*
Fat is hidden in many foods, sweet and savoury. These figures show the percentage of fat in the following products:

	Fat percentage
Liver sausage	27
Salami	45
Pork pie	27
Sausage roll (flaky pastry)	36
Frozen potato chips (fries), fried	19
Potato crisps (chips)	36
Roasted, salted peanuts	49
Mayonnaise	79
Chocolate coated biscuits (cookies)	28
Chocolate éclair	24
Doughnut	16
Mince pie	21
Double (heavy) cream	48
Cream cheese	48
Milk chocolate	30

Table 4: *Foods to Choose and Foods to Avoid*

Foods to choose

White fish — cod, plaice (flounder), haddock, etc.
Oily fish — mackerel, herring, etc.
Shellfish — prawns, shrimps, etc.
Poultry — chicken, turkey
Game — rabbit, pheasant, duck
Skimmed milk and skimmed milk products such as yogurt, soft cheeses and those made with low-fat milks
Whole wheat products — flour, pasta, bread
Whole grain foods — buckwheat, oats, brown rice, unpolished pearl (pot) barley, etc.
Pulses (legumes) — beans, peas and lentils
Nuts and seeds — in moderation
Fresh fruits
Fresh vegetables
Limited quantities of vegetable oils and vegetable margarines high in polyunsaturated fatty acids
Eggs — limited use only.

Foods to avoid

Red meats — pork, beef, lamb
Meat products — pies, sausages, processed meats
Hard cheeses — Cheddar (New York Cheddar), etc.
Full-fat milk and full-fat milk products
Cream — single (light), double (heavy), whipping and clotted
Ice-cream
Processed cakes and biscuits (cookies)
Snack foods — crisps (chips) and other savouries
Fried foods
Butter, lard, dripping
Chocolate

The Recipes

All the recipes in this book bear an approximate fat and calorie value. These have been calculated from McCance and Widdowson's *The Composition of Foods*. All recipes have been designed with a low level of saturated fat in mind. Because our bodies need some fat, that which is polyunsaturated from vegetable sources, some recipes include small amounts of oils such as sunflower, corn, soya, or safflower that supply these vital fatty acids. Olive oil is included in some recipes for its flavour and it too contributes some of the important polyunsaturated fatty acids. Where recipes require vegetables to be sautéed for flavour this can be carried out using a small amount of vegetable stock or alternatively a combination of stock and oil. For convenience I make a quantity of stock and freeze it in ice cube trays. Individual cubes can then be taken out when required. Alternatively, in recipes where vegetable stock is being used anyway, e.g. soups, use 1 tablespoon of the stock for sautéing. Where recipes use oil for sautéing, stock can be substituted for a lower calorie and fat value — but do remember that a small amount of vegetable oil is needed to supply vital fatty acids (see page 10 for full explanation).

Chapter 3

Breakfasts

Breakfast like a king . . . so the saying goes. Today we all seem to be too rushed to take the time to sit down and eat a reasonable breakfast. For most families breakfast is a time of hurried greetings, a quick cup of coffee and then a rush for the door. A couple of hours later hunger strikes and that means a dash out for some chocolate, a Danish pastry . . . To avoid those mid-morning hunger pangs, learn to start the day sensibly — at home with a proper breakfast. For most people the notion of a 'proper' breakfast conjures up platefuls of over-greasy fried foods — not surprisingly, few people nowadays indulge in them. There are alternatives, however, that will provide the body with fuel to see it through the morning until lunch-time and do not rely on large helpings of fat.

The importance of adequate fibre in the diet has already been mentioned and choosing wholemeal (whole wheat) bread in place of white sliced bread is the best way to start overhauling your fibre intake. In a diet where fat needs to be restricted, however, take care not to be too heavy-handed with the butter. Choose instead a soft vegetable oil-based margarine that is labelled high in polyunsaturated fatty acids and use sparingly. Be more generous, however, with your chosen topping — honey, sugar-free fruit jam (jelly), marmalade, yeast extract or some peanut butter. Croissants are a lovely treat but are forbidden to the fat-conscious; all those lovely layers are there because of the vast quantities of fat used in the baking! If you're bored at the prospect of plain wholemeal (whole wheat) toast every day why not ring the changes with some of the more unusual breads available. There are good whole grain breads on sale that are really nutritious, retaining the full value of the cereal grain in its unprocessed state. Try your hand at baking your own loaves, too, (see page 97). It's hard to beat the smell of freshly baked bread and with just a little practice it is possible to turn out top-quality loaves and rolls each time.

Breakfast cereals are another valuable source of energy and can boost the intake of fibre, vitamins and minerals if they are based on unrefined whole grains. Avoid highly processed cereals with large quantities of sugar added. Watch out for the salt content — many cereals contain a surprisingly high quantity. Oat-based breakfast cereals are probably the wisest choice for those concerned with eating for a healthier heart. Oats contain a higher level of soluble fibre than other cereals, hence the arrival on the market of products from the big manufacturers linking oats to preventing heart disease. To benefit from oat fibre, though, it is not essential to eat these speciality products — good old-fashioned porridge will boost your intake of this valuable soluble fibre, too. Follow the recipe on page 27 for a tasty fat-conscious muesli mixture.

Many traditional breakfasts are based on eggs. As already noted, eggs should be eaten in moderation because of the high level of saturated fat they contain, yet, there is a place for up to three eggs a week in the diet and in dishes like Breakfast Kedgeree (see page 30) it is possible to reduce the amount of eggs and still end up with a tasty dish. Dishes where eggs are the major ingredient, however, are less easy to adapt and are best omitted altogether. Instead of hot egg dishes, try grilled (broiled) tomatoes served with lightly poached mushrooms, and, if you must, a very lean rasher of grilled (broiled) bacon.

For everyday breakfasts, home-made yogurt is a cheap and nutritious dish that can be served in many ways with fresh or dried fruits. For liquid refreshment choose fruit juices, herb teas or varieties of teas such as Ceylon that are low in tannin. Decaffeinated coffee is also preferable to standard coffee and there are many respectable blends now available, both instant and ground, to make this a pleasant substitute. Remember to add skimmed milk to your hot drinks in place of full-fat milk — or drink them black.

Yogurt

There are many different types of natural yogurt now available. For least fat and calories, choose products that are made from skimmed milk as these contain only traces of fat. If in doubt, make your own — it is not difficult. The golden rules are, first, not to add the milk at such a high temperature that it destroys the bacteria and, second, to leave the yogurt long enough to incubate, so the bacteria can do their trick and turn plain milk into the refreshing tanginess of natural yogurt at a fraction of the price of shop brands.

There are many yogurt makers on the market, but cheapest of all is the wide-necked *Thermos* flask. However you might like to buy a model with individual cartons as these are convenient for transporting and children like to have their own pot of yogurt.

Own Mix Muesli

While it's nice to have lots of nuts to chew on in your morning muesli, too many will raise the fat level dramatically. Mix your own muesli using hazelnuts, which are less fatty than the more usual almonds and walnuts. Add plenty of dried fruit and choose jumbo-sized oat flakes.

Supplies 6.3g fat and 230 calories per portion.

Imperial/metric	Serves 12	American
1 lb (450g)	jumbo-sized oat flakes	4 cups
4 oz (100g)	sultanas/golden seedless raisins	⅔ cup
2 oz (50g)	raisins	⅔ cup
2 oz (50g)	dates	scant ½ cup
2 oz (50g)	dried apricots	scant ½ cup
4 oz (100g)	hazelnuts	¾ cup
	pinch of nutmeg	
¼ tsp	ground cinnamon	¼ tsp

1 Put the oat flakes in a bowl and stir in the sultanas (golden seedless raisins) and raisins.
2 Chop the dates, apricots and hazelnuts and stir into the bowl.
3 Add the spices and mix all the ingredients together thoroughly.
4 Store in an air-tight container. Serve with skimmed milk, yogurt, orange or apple juice and, add some chopped fresh fruit if desired.

Natural Yogurt

Yogurt is a versatile food, particularly so in a low-fat diet. Its distinctive taste makes it an ideal addition to salads and sauces where it adds depth of flavour without greatly increasing the fat value of the dish. Like the skimmed milk from which it is made, natural yogurt is valuable for its protein content, which helps to balance the protein found in plant sources — grains, pulses (legumes) and nuts and seeds. It also supplies calcium as well as useful amounts of B vitamins.

Yogurt is an excellent breakfast food. There are countless ways of brightening up a bowl of natural yogurt. Add fresh fruit for valuable vitamin C as well as fibre or dried fruits, which are not such good sources of the former but are excellent foods for boosting fibre intake.

Supplies 0.8g fat and 260 calories.

Imperial/metric	*Makes 1 pt (600ml/2 cups)*	American
1 pt (600ml)	skimmed milk	2 cups
1 tbs	natural/unsweetened yogurt	1 tbs
1 tbs	skimmed milk powder	1 tbs

1 Put the milk in a saucepan and heat to 110°F/50°C.

2 While the milk is warming, mix the yogurt and skimmed milk powder together and spoon into the bottom of a wide-necked *Thermos* flask or yogurt maker.

3 Pour the heated milk into the flask and stir in thoroughly to distribute the yogurt mixture (the 'starter') evenly. Cover and leave to incubate for 6–8 hours. Release the lid, and chill until required.

Here are a few ideas for breakfast-time yogurt treats. All use ¼ pt (150ml/⅔ cup) of natural (unsweetened) yogurt as a base.

Banana Swirl mash a banana and stir it into the yogurt with some seedless white grapes.

Honeyed Prune soak overnight 2 oz (50g/scant ½ cup) prunes, then chop and stir into the yogurt with 1 tsp clear honey.

Peach Dream chop up one ripe peach and stir it into the yogurt. Top with 1 tbs muesli.

Spiced Delight grate one eating (dessert) apple into the yogurt and stir in a pinch of ground nutmeg and a little ground cinnamon.

Raisin Glory chop one eating (dessert) apple into the yogurt and stir in 1 tbs raisins.

Orange Extravaganza chop a peeled orange into the yogurt and add 1 tbs wheatgerm.

Melon Moments dice a peeled portion of melon into the yogurt and add a few sliced strawberries.

Apricot Tang soak overnight 2 oz (50g/scant ½ cup) dried apricots, then chop and add to the yogurt 2 tsp flaked (slivered) almonds.

Grapefruit Boat chop a peeled half a grapefruit, mix with the yogurt and 1 tbs sultanas (golden seedless raisins) and pile back into the grapefruit half.

Gingered Melon dice a peeled melon slice and mix into the yogurt with a pinch of ground ginger.

Dried Fruit Compote

Remember to prepare this in the evening so that next morning the fruit will be plump and spicy. Choose your own selection of dried fruits.

Supplies a trace of fat and 160 calories per portion.

Imperial/metric	Serves 4	American
¾ pt (450ml)	cold water	2 cups
1	lemon, thinly sliced	1
1	orange, thinly sliced	1
2-in (5-cm)	cinnamon stick	2-in
¾ lb (325g)	mixture of prunes, dried apricots, dried pears, apple rings, etc.	2½ cups

1 Pour the water into a pan. Add the lemon and orange slices to the pan with the cinnamon. Bring to the boil and simmer for 2 minutes.

2 Pour the strained liquid over the fruit of your choice, add the cinnamon and leave to soak overnight. Remove the cinnamon before serving.

Breakfast Kedgeree

This recipe contains fewer eggs than most conventional kedgerees to keep the fat level down. Arbroath smokies are free of colourings.

Supplies 8.4g fat and 350 calories per portion.

Imperial/metric	Serves 4	American
1 lb (450g)	smoked haddock *or* Arbroath smokies	1 lb
1	bay leaf	1
½ lb (225g)	long grain brown rice	1 cup
2 oz (50g)	button mushrooms, chopped	1 cup
2	free-range eggs	2
2 tbs	skimmed milk	2 tbs
	freshly ground black pepper	
2 tbs	fresh parsley, chopped	2 tbs

1 Put the fish in a pan with enough cold water to just cover. Poach over a low heat for 10–12 minutes until the flesh is just firm.

2 Remove the fish from the pan. Pour the cooking fluid into a jug and make up to 18 fl oz (540ml/2⅓ cups) with cold water.

3 Pour the stock into a pan and add the bay leaf, rice and mushrooms. Bring to the boil, then reduce the heat and simmer for 25–30 minutes until the rice is just soft and most of the stock has been absorbed. While the rice is cooking, hard-boil (hard-cook) the eggs.

4 Flake the fish, chop the eggs and add to the rice with the skimmed milk. Heat gently until the milk is absorbed. Season to taste with freshly ground black pepper and serve garnished with the parsley.

Chapter 4

Healthy Lunch Breaks

Whenever we have to find food in a hurry we tend to pile on the fat. Lunch-time for most people means a hurried sandwich grabbed from the local bakers or a hasty hamburger from the nearest take-away. Instant food is often loaded with fat: burger and fries, Chinese take-aways, doner kebabs (kabobs) and the like all hide fat. If lunch is taken at home then there's always the temptation to fix a fry-up — it's quick and easy. If you're concerned about the amount of fat in your diet then you need to start afresh to make sure that the hungry hour in the middle of the day doesn't undo the good you're doing elsewhere.

Here are a few suggestions to help you on your way.

Sandwiches

Sandwiches are the obvious choice for a lunch-box and for lunch eaten at home, too. Try to be mean with the margarine when spreading it on your bread. Choose a brand that is high in polyunsaturated fatty acids and spread it thinly. Avoid the temptation of egg mayonnaise, cheese or ham — all fat fiends! Choose instead plenty of salad ingredients, low-fat soft cheese, peanut butter, prawns (large shrimp), canned salmon. Be adventurous and ring the changes by eating wholemeal (whole wheat) rolls or pitta bread every once in a while.

Here are some tried and tested favourites:

- low-fat soft cheese mashed with banana
- low-fat soft cheese with pineapple and beansprouts
- grated apple tossed with yogurt, chopped celery and raisins
- peanut butter with tomato and lettuce or alfalfa sprouts
- cooked chicken diced with avocado and yogurt
- shredded lettuce, chopped peppers, diced cucumber and tomato slices.

Don't forget open sandwiches. Choose either a crispbread or bread such as rye or Pumpernickel. Arrange your chosen topping attractively and serve it fresh before the base becomes soft. Try:

- tahini and cucumber with alfalfa sprouts
- low-fat soft cheese and orange segments
- button mushrooms and prawns (large shrimp)
- baby beetroot (beets) with sliced green pepper (sweet green pepper) and kiwi fruit
- soused herring with lettuce
- avocado and orange
- tomato slices, olives and pepper strips

Baked potatoes

Potatoes cooked in their jackets are very popular as a substantial snack but they are often served with fat-rich goodies such as sour cream and grated cheese. If you're a baked potato fan, there is no reason why you can't still enjoy them, but go easy on the topping. Begin by substituting the lavish butter for a small amount of PUFA-rich margarine and choose low-fat soft cheese topped with low-fat ingredients.

To cook the perfect potato, pre-heat the oven to 400°F/200°C (Gas Mark 6); select good-quality potatoes, allowing each person a potato weighing 6–8 oz (175–225g); wash them well to remove any surface dirt and prick all over with a fork, (there is no need to rub either fat or oil into the skin — although this is often recommended, I find that potatoes bake perfectly well without either); place them spaced apart on the top shelf of the oven and leave to cook for 1¼ hours until the skins are crispy and the flesh soft. Give the potatoes a gentle squeeze — wearing oven gloves to protect yourself from the heat of the oven — to see if they are done.

Here are a few low-fat toppings:

- *cottage (pot) cheese and pineapple*: for each person allow 2 oz (50g/2 tbs) cottage (pot) cheese and chop 2 rings of pineapple, canned in natural juice, and arrange on top of the baked potato. Sprinkle with fresh, chopped parsley.

- *low-fat soft cheese and herbs*: allow 2 oz (50g/2 tbs) of low-fat soft cheese for each potato and mix with 1 tbs fresh chopped chives and 1 tsp chopped parsley (alternatively, finely chop 2 spring onions (scallions) and mix with parsley or add 3 tbs sweetcorn kernels)

- *Italian tomato*: chop a quarter of an onion and sauté in a smear of vegetable oil, stir in 2 chopped tomatoes (canned or fresh) and a sprinkling of dried oregano, then pile on top of the baked potato with a few strips of green pepper (sweet green pepper) and some parsley on top

- *mushrooms*: allow 3 oz (75g/1½ cups) button mushrooms per person, chop them finely and poach in a little vegetable stock with a squeeze of lemon juice added, then season generously with pepper and pile on top of the potato, then top this with a swirl of natural (unsweetened) yogurt and garnish with parsley.

Soups

Soups are ideal for lunch-time as, served with wholemeal (whole wheat) bread, they are filling and sustaining. Some soups take only a short time to make and can be prepared quickly, while others, needing more lengthy cooking, can be made the night before and simply reheated when required. Because they can be carried in *Thermos* flasks, soups are useful for lunches eaten away from home and are especially warming on cold winter days. Don't dismiss soups during summer months, though, as they can be equally refreshing when made with the lighter vegetables of summer and can, if liked, be served chilled. Try some of the delicious recipes in this chapter and you'll see just how simple they are to make and so much tastier than canned soup.

Salads

Just as soups need not be confined to the winter months, salads should form an important part of your diet throughout the year. There are almost endless variations on 'the salad' — gone are the days when most people conjured with just lettuce, cucumber and tomato. Now all manner of vegetables, fruits, nuts, seeds, pulses (legumes) and grains, as well as animal foods, are used in salads. In this chapter are just a few recipes that are perfect for lunch. Slightly more substantial than side salads, which are designed to accompany other dishes, the six salads included all contain protein-based foods. The salads are accompanied by a selection of low-fat dressings. Oils, such as olive and sunflower have been used for their nutritional properties as well as flavouring, but unnecessarily fatty dressings such as mayonnaise have been omitted. Many salads can be packed up in air-tight boxes for picnics or to brighten up any lunch-time at the office.

French Bread Pizzas

A quick alternative to traditional pizzas. The topping can be varied to include favourite foods.

Supplies 4.2g fat and 430 calories per portion.

Imperial/metric	Serves 4	American
8 slices	wholemeal/whole wheat French bread	8 slices
	For the topping:	
8 tbs	tomato purée/paste with herbs	8 tbs
1	green pepper/sweet green pepper, deseeded and chopped	1
3 oz (75g)	mushrooms, sliced	1½ cups
3 tbs	sweetcorn kernels	3 tbs
4	olives, halved and pitted	4
	freshly ground black pepper	

1 Put the French bread on a baking tray (sheet) and spread a tablespoon of the tomato purée (paste) on each piece.
2 Arrange the pepper and mushrooms on top of the bread with the sweetcorn and halved olives.

3 Put them under a very hot grill (broiler) for 3–5 minutes or, if you already have the oven hot, put them on the top shelf of the oven and bake for 10 minutes. Serve hot with a green salad.

Pitta Bread

Supplies 2.7g fat and 375 calories each.

Imperial/metric	Makes 6	American
¾ lb (325g)	wholemeal/whole wheat flour	3 cups
1 tsp	sea salt	1 tsp
1 oz (25g)	fresh yeast	2½ tbs
2 tsp	olive oil	2 tsp
1 tsp	honey	1 tsp
8 fl oz (240ml)	lukewarm water	1 cup

1 Put the flour and salt in a mixing bowl. Crumble the yeast into a jug and add the oil, honey and water. Stir until the yeast has dissolved and then pour onto the flour.

2 Mix the flour and yeast mixture together with your hands to form a dough.

3 Put the dough on to a lightly floured surface and knead for 10 minutes until smooth. Put it back into the bowl and cover. Leave to prove (rise) in a warm place until it has doubled in size.

4 Divide the dough into six pieces, (it is essential that pitta bread is rolled thinly and baked at the top of a hot oven so, unless you own a fan oven where the distribution of heat is even throughout, it is best to place one half of the dough in the fridge to rest (let stand) and bake the pitta bread in two batches). Roll each piece of dough into a ball and flatten each ball slightly so it makes an oval shape, ¼-in (0.5-cm) thick.

5 Slide the ovals onto baking trays (sheets) and dust the top with a little flour. Cover and leave to prove (rise) in a warm place for 20 minutes.

6 Set the oven to 450°F/230°C (Gas Mark 8). Put empty trays (baking sheets) in the oven to heat through and when the pitta bread has proved (risen) slide the bread onto these hot trays (sheets). Bake at the top of the oven for 10 minutes.

7 Remove from the oven and leave to cool on a wire cooling rack before cutting in half and filling.

Courgette (Zucchini) Cooler

Even if you don't serve this chilled, somehow the refreshing taste of courgettes (zucchini) helps to cool hot heads!

Supplies 1.2g fat and 46 calories per portion.

Imperial/metric	Serves 4	American
1 tsp	sunflower oil	1 tsp
2 oz (50g)	onion, chopped	⅓ cup
¾ lb (325g)	courgettes/zucchini, diced	5 cups
3 oz (75g)	potato, scrubbed and diced	½ cup
1¼ pt (750ml)	chicken or vegetable stock	3 cups
1	bay leaf	1
	freshly ground black pepper	
small pot	natural/unsweetened yogurt (optional)	small pot

1 Put the oil in the pan and add the onion. Stir over a low heat for a minute before adding the courgettes (zucchini), potato, stock and bay leaf.
2 Bring the contents of the pan to the boil, reduce the heat and simmer for 20 minutes. Remove the bay leaf.

3 Liquidize (blend) the soup, return it to the pan and season to taste with freshly ground black pepper. Reheat if serving warm or leave to cool, then chill if serving cold. Serve with swirls of yogurt and a few thin slices of courgette (zucchini) if liked.

Parsnip Potage

Parsnips replace the traditional leeks in this tasty version of the classic chilled vichyssoise.

Supplies 1.5g fat and 120 calories.

Imperial/metric	Serves 4	American
1 tsp	sunflower oil	1 tsp
2	frozen cubes vegetable stock	2
1 large	onion, chopped	1 large
½ lb (225g)	parsnips, peeled and chopped	1⅓ cups
¾ lb (325g)	potatoes, scrubbed and diced	2 cups
¼ tsp	thyme, dried	¼ tsp
2	bay leaves	2
1¼ pt (750ml)	vegetable stock	3 cups
⅛ pt (150ml)	skimmed milk	⅔ cup
	freshly ground black pepper	
	parsley to garnish	

1 Put the oil and frozen cubes of stock in a pan and heat gently. Add the prepared vegetables and cook for 1 minute.

2 Add the thyme, bay leaves, stock and skimmed milk and bring to the boil. Reduce the heat and simmer for 40 minutes until all the vegetables are tender.

3 Remove the bay leaves, liquidize (blend) the soup and reheat, seasoning to taste with freshly ground black pepper. Serve garnished with parsley.

Lentil Soup

A protein-packed soup, the protein is made complete by the addition of a wholemeal (whole wheat) roll. Indian spices add zest.

Supplies 1.5g fat and 130 calories per portion.

Imperial/metric	Serves 4	American
1 large	onion, chopped	1 large
4 oz (100g)	carrot, scrubbed and diced	⅔ cup
1 tsp	sunflower oil	1 tsp
2	frozen cubes vegetable stock	2
¼ tsp	turmeric	¼ tsp
¼ tsp	ground cumin	¼ tsp
pinch	cayenne pepper	pinch
5 oz (150g)	red lentils	¾ cup
1½ pt (900ml)	vegetable stock	3¾ cups
1	bay leaf	1
	freshly ground black pepper	

1 Cook the onion and carrot gently in the oil and frozen stock cubes over a low heat for 1 minute and stir in the turmeric, cumin and cayenne pepper and cook for a further minute.

2 Add the lentils, vegetable stock and bay leaf, bring to the boil, then reduce the heat and simmer for 30 minutes until the lentils are quite soft.

3 Remove the bay leaf, liquidize (blend) the soup and reheat, seasoning to taste with freshly ground black pepper.

Country Vegetable Soup

The vegetables used in this soup can be varied according to what's available.

Supplies 0.4g fat and 95 calories per portion.

Imperial/metric	Serves 4	American
1 tsp	olive oil	1 tsp
2	frozen cubes vegetable stock	2
1 large	onion, finely chopped	1 large
1	clove garlic, crushed/minced	1
2	celery stalks/sticks finely chopped	2
4 oz (100g)	carrot, scrubbed and diced	⅔ cup
4 oz (100g)	potato, scrubbed and diced	⅔ cup
4 oz (100g)	swede/rutabaga, peeled and diced	⅔ cup
1½ pt (900ml)	vegetable stock	3¾ cups
2 tbs	tomato purée/paste	2 tbs
2	bay leaves	2
pinch	thyme	pinch
3 oz (75g)	haricot/navy beans, soaked overnight	scant ½ cup
3 oz (75g)	white cabbage, finely shredded	¾ cup
	freshly ground black pepper	
3 tbs	fresh parsley, chopped	3 tbs

1 Heat the oil and frozen stock in a large saucepan over a low heat and stir in the prepared vegetables.
2 Add the stock, tomato purée (paste), bay leaves, thyme and drained beans. Bring to the boil, reduce the heat and simmer for 1 hour, until the beans are almost tender.
3 Stir in the shredded cabbage and continue to cook for 10 minutes. Season to taste with freshly ground black pepper and stir in the parsley. Serve hot.

Creamy Mushroom Soup

It's hard to believe that this soup is made from skimmed milk — the result is beautifully smooth and creamy to taste.

Supplies 1.8g fat and 70 calories per portion.

Imperial/metric	Serves 4	American
2 oz (50g)	onion, finely chopped	⅓ cup
4 oz (100g)	potato, scrubbed and diced	⅔ cup
1 tsp	sunflower oil	1 tsp
10 oz (275g)	button mushrooms, chopped	4 cups
½ tsp dried	thyme	½ tsp dried
or 1 tsp fresh		*or* 1 tsp fresh
¾ pt (450ml)	skimmed milk	2 cups
½ pt (300ml)	vegetable *or* chicken stock	1⅓ cups
1	bay leaf	1
	freshly ground black pepper	
	parsley or chives, chopped, to garnish	

1 Cook the onion and potato gently in the oil for 1 minute.

2 Add the mushrooms, thyme, skimmed milk, stock and bay leaf. Bring to the boil, then reduce the heat and simmer for 25 minutes.

3 Remove the bay leaf, liquidize (blend) the soup, reheat, seasoning to taste with freshly ground black pepper and serve garnished with the parsley or chives.

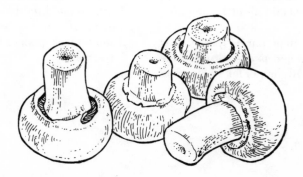

Mediterranean Salad

Supplies 6.4g fat and 200 calories per portion.

Imperial/metric	Serves 4	American
¾ lb (325g)	French/fine green beans	¾ cup
5 oz (150g)	wholemeal/whole wheat pasta shells	3 cups
1 tbs	olive oil	1 tbs
½	lemon, juice of	½
½ tsp dried	oregano	½ tsp dried
or 1 tsp fresh		*or* 1 tsp fresh
	freshly ground black pepper	
3	tomatoes, ripe, chopped	3
1	green pepper/sweet green pepper, deseeded and chopped	1
2 oz (50g)	button mushrooms, sliced	¾ cup
6	black ripe olives, halved and pitted	6

1 Trim the French (fine green) beans and steam or boil in a little water for 5–8 minutes until just tender. Drain.

2 While they are cooking, plunge the pasta into boiling water and cook for 10–12 minutes.

3 Have ready a screw-top jar with the olive oil, lemon juice, oregano and a little freshly ground black pepper shaken together well in it. Drain the pasta, and toss with the beans in a salad bowl, then shake the dressing once more and pour it over the beans and pasta.

4 Add the tomatoes, pepper (sweet green pepper) and mushrooms to the bowl.

5 Decorate with the olives and serve when the pasta and beans have chilled.

Hawaiian Rice Salad

Vegetarians can omit the prawns (large shrimp) and still enjoy this tasty salad.

Supplies 0.5g fat and 100 calories per portion.

Imperial/metric	Serves 4	American
6 oz (175g)	long grain brown rice	⅔ cup
2 oz (50g)	button mushrooms, chopped	¾ cup
1	red pepper/sweet red pepper, deseeded and chopped	1
4	pineapple rings, canned in natural juice, drained and chopped	4
4 oz (100g)	prawns/large shrimp, peeled	4 oz
2	bananas	2
1 tbs	chives, chopped	1 tbs
	freshly ground black pepper	

1 Put the rice in a pan with ¾ pt (450ml/2 cups) cold water. Cook until almost soft, then add the chopped mushrooms to the pan. Turn off the heat and let the mushrooms and rice finish cooking in the steam. When the rice is ready, pour it into a salad bowl.

2 Add the pepper and pineapple to the rice with the prawns (large shrimp) and let the mixture cool.

3 When mixture is cold, slice the bananas into the bowl and add the chives. Season with freshly ground black pepper, toss together and serve.

Caraway Coleslaw

If you don't like the taste of caraway, substitute a little dried thyme in its place.

Under ½g fat and 45 calories per portion.

Imperial/metric	Serves 4	American
½ lb (225g)	carrots, scrubbed and grated	1⅓ cups
½ lb (225g)	white cabbage, finely shredded	2 cups
3	spring onions/scallions	3
2	eating/dessert apples	2
3 tbs	natural/unsweetened yogurt	3 tbs
½ tsp *or* ¼ tsp	caraway seeds *or* dried thyme	½ tsp *or* ¼ tsp
1 tbs	fresh parsley, chopped	1 tbs
	freshly ground black pepper	

1 Put the grated carrots in a bowl. Add the cabbage and mix the two together.

2 Trim the spring onions (scallions) and cut them into fine rings. Add them to the carrot and cabbage.

3 Grate the apples — discarding the core — and add to the bowl. Pour the yogurt and sprinkle the caraway seeds or thyme and parsley over and stir. Season with freshly ground black pepper and serve.

Beanshoot and Banana Salad

Supplies 9g fat and 170 calories per portion.

Imperial/metric	Serves 4	American
6 oz (175g)	carrots, scrubbed and grated	1 cup
1	red pepper/sweet red pepper, deseeded and chopped	1
2 handsful	beanshoots/beansprouts	2 handsful
2 oz (50g)	peanuts	½ cup
2 oz (50g)	sultanas/golden seedless raisins	⅓ cup
2	bananas	2
½	lemon, juice of	½
1 tbs	sunflower oil	1 tbs
pinch	paprika	pinch
	freshly ground black pepper	

1 Mix together the carrots, pepper (sweet pepper), beanshoots (beansprouts), peanuts and sultanas (golden seedless raisins) in a bowl.
2 Peel the bananas and slice finely into the salad bowl.

3 In a screw-top jar, put the lemon juice, oil, paprika and a little freshly ground black pepper. Shake vigorously and pour over the salad. Serve at once.

Creamy Cumin Salad

Supplies 0.5g fat and 160 calories per portion.

Imperial/metric	Serves 4	American
5 oz (150g)	wholemeal/whole wheat macaroni	3 cups
2	red eating/dessert apples	2
	lemon juice	
4-in (10cm)	cucumber, finely diced	4-in piece
1	green pepper/sweet green pepper, deseeded and chopped	1
3 tbs	low-fat yogurt	3 tbs
¾ tsp	cumin seeds, ground	¾ tsp
pinch	cayenne pepper	pinch
	freshly ground black pepper	

1 Plunge the pasta into boiling water and cook for 10–12 minutes until almost soft. Drain and set aside.

2 Peel, core and dice the apples. Toss the apples in a little lemon juice to prevent them browning.

3 Mix the pasta with the prepared vegetables and apples in a bowl and pour over the yogurt, cumin, cayenne pepper and season with a little freshly ground black pepper. Chill before serving.

Chicken and Celery Toss

Supplies 2.4g fat and 180 calories per portion.

Imperial/metric	Serves 4	American
10 oz (275g)	chicken, cooked	10 oz
4	celery sticks/stalks, finely chopped	4
2 oz (50g)	raisins	⅓ cup
1	green pepper/sweet green pepper, deseeded and finely chopped	1
2 tbs	low-fat yogurt	2 tbs
2 tbs	low-fat soft cheese	2 tbs
few drops	*Tabasco* sauce	few drops
generous pinch	cayenne pepper	generous pinch
	freshly ground black pepper	
	crisp lettuce, shredded	

1 Cut the chicken into bite-sized pieces. Mix the celery and the raisins together with the chicken.
2 Add the pepper (sweet pepper) to the other ingredients.
3 In a separate bowl, blend the yogurt, the soft cheese, *Tabasco*, cayenne pepper and a little freshly ground black pepper together. Pour this mixture over the salad and toss thoroughly. Serve on a bed of the shredded lettuce. Wholemeal (whole wheat) bread is an ideal accompaniment.

Chapter 5

Main Courses

The main meal of the day is also the most important. At this meal we consume more food and so obtain more nutrients than any other. The success of a low-fat diet is very much determined by the type of food eaten as the main meal each evening or lunch-time. Obviously we have to watch out for hidden fat at breakfast and lighter meals and snacks, but it is important to make sure that the day's main course is as low in fat as possible.

This chapter includes a wide range of recipes designed for everyday use. Chapter 8, Entertaining Ideas, includes dishes that have that 'something special' to impress guests but there's no reason why many of the more economical dishes found in this chapter cannot also be used for entertaining.

One of the keys to a successful diet is variety and in this section there are many simple ideas that can be altered to create different dishes. Most recipes are vegetarian but for those not wanting to cut out animal foods altogether there are also recipes that contain poultry or fish and

are low in fat. Surprisingly, lentils are an excellent alternative to mince (ground round), and are just as versatile as this standby favourite. Using these small round brown lentils in place of minced beef in Bolognese-type sauces produces a tasty sauce that can be used with pasta, rice, as a stuffing or, as it appears here, in Shepherdess Pie (page 66).

Other members of the pulse (legume) family are also valuable in low-fat main meals. There are many varieties of beans in many shapes, sizes and colours. Used whole or cooked and mashed to a purée they can form the basis of many dishes for winter and summer meals. Different types of grain are also valuable as substitutes for rice to ring the changes.

Stocks

Home-made stocks win hands down for flavour but can be time-consuming to make. However, once the ingredients have been prepared, the stock needs little attention and can be left alone to cook slowly — or can be cooked faster in a pressure cooker. Remember to strain the stock and leave it to cool so that any fat can be skimmed off and discarded. Freeze the stock in ice cube trays for use in recipes in place of traditional fat or oil, or use as a tasty base for soups, sauces and casseroles. There are many excellent stock (bouillon) cubes now available but watch out for hidden salt. Choose low-salt vegetable stock (bouillon) cubes available from health food stores in preference to those high in artificial additives and salt. Stock (bouillon) cubes can also be made up into stock and frozen in ice cube trays for later use. Make sure other members of the family know which ice cubes in the freezer are frozen stock and which are water!

Sauces for Spaghetti

One of the simplest supper dishes is spaghetti topped with a tasty sauce. Choose wholemeal (whole wheat) spaghetti because, made from wholemeal (whole wheat) rather than white flour, it contains more fibre, vitamins and minerals. It has a slightly nutty flavour. The same cooking rules apply to both wholemeal (whole wheat) and white spaghetti — plunge it into boiling water and fork through to prevent it sticking. Cook until *al dente*, that is, until almost soft, but with a little bite remaining. Many sauces for pasta can be made the day before and quickly reheated or can be frozen and thawed out before use.

Chicken Stock

Imperial/metric	*Makes 2 pts/1.1 litres/5 cups*	American
1	chicken carcass	1
2 pts (1.2 l)	water	5 cups
1	onion, roughly chopped	1
4 oz (100g)	carrots, scrubbed and diced	⅓ cup
1	celery stick/stalk, chopped	1
2	bay leaves	2
6	black peppercorns	6
1 sprig *or* ½ tsp	thyme, fresh *or* dried	1 sprig *or* ½ tsp

1 Put the chicken carcass in a large saucepan with the water.

2 Add the prepared vegetables to the pan with the bay leaves, peppercorns and thyme.

3 Bring to the boil, then reduce the heat and simmer, covered, for 1½ hours over a very low heat. Alternatively, pressure cook for 25 minutes at 15 lb (6 kilos) pressure.

4 When the stock is ready, strain it and leave it to cool. When it is cold, skim off the fat. The stock is now ready to use straight away or to freeze.

Vegetable Stock

Imperial/metric	*Makes 2 pts/1.1 litres/5 cups*	American
1	celery stick/stalk, chopped	1
1	onion, chopped	1
4 oz (100g)	carrots, scrubbed and diced	⅓ cup
6	black peppercorns	6
1 sprig *or* ¾ tsp	thyme, fresh *or* dried	1 sprig *or* ½ tsp
3	parsley stalks/stems	3
2 pts /1.2 l)	water	5 cups

1 Put all the vegetables in a large saucepan with the peppercorns, thyme, parsley stalks (stems) and water and bring to the boil.

2 Reduce the heat and simmer slowly for 1–1¼ hours. Alternatively, pressure cook at 15 lb (6 kilos) pressure for 15 minutes.

3 Strain the stock and leave to cool. Then you can either use it that day or freeze it in ice cube trays.

Court Bouillon

This special stock is ideal for poaching fish.

Imperial/metric	*Makes 2 pts/1.1 litres/5 cups*	American
1	carrot, scrubbed and diced	1
1	onion, chopped	1
1	celery stick/stalk, chopped	1
1	bay leaf	1
2	sprigs thyme	2
3	parsley stalks/stems	3
½	lemon, juice of	½
¼ pt (150ml)	dry white wine	⅔ cup
¾ pt (450ml)	water	2 cups
6	black peppercorns	6

1 Put the vegetables in a large saucepan with the remaining ingredients. Cover and bring to the boil. Reduce the heat and simmer for 20 minutes.
2 Leave to cool before straining and then use to poach fish.

Note: Salmon, turbot and halibut as well as more economical white fish (cod, plaice (flounder), haddock) are all excellent poached gently either in the oven or over a low heat on the hob until just firm. Never over-poach fish or cook at too high a temperature as the flesh will become hard and tough.

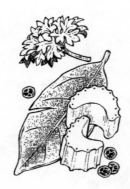

Fish Cooked with Potatoes and Yogurt

Supplies 3g fat and 300 calories per portion.

Imperial/metric	Serves 4	American
1 tsp	olive oil	1 tsp
2	frozen cubes stock	2
1	onion, finely chopped	1
1	clove garlic, crushed/minced	1
2 tbs	tomato purée/paste	2 tbs
¾ pt (425ml)	water	2 cups
¼ pt (150ml)	dry/hard cider *or* vegetable stock	⅔ cup
2	bay leaves	2
pinch	basil	pinch
pinch	cayenne pepper	pinch
1 lb (450g)	potatoes, scrubbed and sliced	1 lb
1½ lb (675g)	cod, haddock or coley, skinned and cut into 1-in (2.5cm) cubes	1½ lb
½ pt (300ml)	low-fat yogurt	1⅓ cups
2 tbs	fresh parsley, chopped	2 tbs
	freshly ground black pepper	

1 Put the oil and stock cubes in a pan and heat gently. Add the onion and garlic and cook for 1 minute.
2 Stir in the tomato purée (paste), water, cider or stock, bay leaves, basil and cayenne pepper. Now add the potatoes.

3 Bring to the boil and simmer for 5 minutes.
4 Add the fish and continue cooking for 15 minutes.
5 Stir in the yogurt and parsley and season to taste with freshly ground black pepper. Cook gently for 3 minutes before serving.

Crispy Topped Plaice (Flounder)

*The addition of a little low-fat hard cheese gives a crispy and tasty
topping.*

Supplies 4.8g fat and 200 calories per portion.

Imperial/metric	Serves 4	American
4 oz (100g)	fresh wholemeal/whole wheat breadcrumbs	2 cups
2 oz (50g)	low-fat Cheddar-style cheese, grated	½ cup
	freshly ground black pepper	
4	plaice/flounder fillets	4
1	lemon, juice of	1

1 In a bowl mix together the breadcrumbs with the cheese and a little freshly ground black pepper to taste.
2 Arrange the fish in a heatproof dish with 1 tsp of cold water in the bottom and pre-heat the grill (broiler) to very hot.

3 Brush the fish with some of the lemon juice and cover with the breadcrumb mixture.
4 Dribble a little more lemon juice over the top and put under the grill (broiler). Cook for 10–12 minutes, turning the heat down if the top becomes too brown. Serve hot.

Baked Fish with Tomatoes

Supplies 4.8g fat and 180 calories per portion.

Imperial/metric	Serves 4	American
8 oz (225g)	onion, finely sliced	1⅓ cups
1 tbs	olive oil	1 tbs
1 large	red or green pepper/sweet red or green pepper, deseeded and sliced	1 large
1 clove	garlic, crushed/minced	1 clove
14-oz (397-g) tin	tomatoes, chopped	14-oz can
1 tbs	tomato purée/paste	1 tbs
1 tsp	dried basil	1 tsp
1¼ lb (550g)	cod or haddock fillet, skinned and cut into 1-in (2.5-cm) cubes freshly ground black pepper	1¼ lb

1 Preheat the oven to 350°F/180°C (Gas Mark 4).

2 Heat the oil in a flameproof casserole dish and add the onion. Cook gently over a low heat for 3 minutes.

3 Stir in the sliced pepper and garlic and cook for a further 2 minutes.

4 Add the tomatoes, tomato purée (paste) and basil. Bring to the boil.

5 Stir in the diced fish, cover and transfer the dish to the preheated oven.

6 Bake for 30 minutes or until the fish is tender. Season generously with freshly ground black pepper and serve with wholemeal (whole wheat) pasta or fresh bread.

Fish and Leek Parcel

Choose good-quality chunky pieces of white fish fillet or steaks for this simple but fresh and delicious dish.

Supplies 3.3g fat and 178 calories per portion.

Imperial/metric	Serves 1	American
6 oz (175g)	white fish fillet or steak	6 oz
	unsalted butter *or* sunflower oil for greasing	
2-in (5-cm) piece	carrot	2-in piece
2-in (5-cm) piece	slim leek, white part	2-in piece
1 tsp	lemon juice, fresh	1 tsp
a few julienne	fresh lemon rind	few matchsticks
1 sprig	fresh parsley, dill or tarragon	1 sprig
	freshly ground black pepper	

1 Wash the fish and pat it dry. Heat the oven to 400°F/200°C (Gas Mark 6). Using butter or oil, lightly grease a 12-in (30-cm) square of greaseproof (waxed) paper.

2 Put the fish in the centre of the paper square. Scrub the carrot and cut it into 12 fine sticks. Cut the leek into 12 similar-width sticks. Arrange on top of the fish, sprinkle the lemon juice, rind and chosen herb over and season with freshly ground black pepper.

3 Fold in the sides of the paper, then roll the edges of the paper together down on top of the fish, but not too tightly.

4 Put the parcel on a baking tray (sheet) and bake for 20–30 minutes, depending on the thickness of the fish. Test after 20 minutes by gently unrolling the paper and piercing the fish with the blade of a knife. The fish should be firm but opaque. Serve the fish in the paper, keeping the juices in. Serve with boiled new potatoes and a green vegetable.

Tuna-stuffed Peppers

Choose dolphin-friendly South Seas tuna for this dish and save fat and calories by buying tuna in brine rather than oil.

Supplies 4.8g fat and 255 calories per portion.

Imperial/metric	*Serves 4*	American
4 medium	peppers/sweet peppers	4 medium
1 tbs	olive oil	1 tbs
4 oz (100g)	onion, finely chopped	⅔ cup
6 oz (175g)	long grain brown rice	¾ cup
8 oz (225g)	button mushrooms, finely chopped	3 cups
15 fl oz (450ml)	vegetable stock or water	2 cups
½ tsp	dried basil	½ tsp
7 oz (210g)	light meat tuna in brine	7 oz
	freshly ground black pepper	

1 Preheat the oven to 375°F/190°C (Gas Mark 5).

2 Slice the tops off the peppers (sweet peppers) and put aside. Using a teaspoon, carefully scoop out the seeds and discard. Plunge the deseeded peppers (sweet peppers) into a pan of boiling water and blanch for 2 minutes. Drain thoroughly and set aside.

3 Heat the olive oil in a large pan and stir in the onion. Cook gently for 1 minute.

4 Stir in the rice, coating it in the oil, then add the mushrooms, stock or water and basil. Bring to the boil then reduce the heat and simmer for 20–25 minutes until the rice is tender and all the liquid has been absorbed.

5 Flake in the tuna and season to taste with freshly ground black pepper.

6 Divide the filling between the peppers (sweet peppers) and smooth the top level. Put the reserved tops back on the peppers (sweet peppers) and arrange them in a shallow ovenproof dish with two or three tbs of water in the bottom. Cover and bake for 25–30 minutes until the peppers (sweet peppers) are tender. Serve with baked potatoes or with a salad for a lighter meal.

Mackerel with Mushrooms

*Although fish like herring and mackerel are higher in fat than white fish,
the type of polyunsaturated fatty acids they contain are thought to help
protect against heart disease. Wrap the prepared fish in foil to let the fish
cook in its own juices, eliminating the need for extra fat. Spring mackerel
are much lower in fat than those caught late in the year. The fat content
varies from 5 per cent to 20 per cent so it is difficult to give a fat and
calorie content for this recipe.*

Imperial/metric	Serves 4	American
4×6-oz (175g)	mackerel, cleaned	4×6-oz
1	lemon, juice of	1
	freshly ground black pepper	
4 oz (100g)	button mushrooms, finely chopped	2 cups
2 tbs	fresh parsley, chopped	2 tbs

1 Wash each fish thoroughly and cut off the heads if you have brought them whole. Preheat the oven to 400°F/200°C (Gas Mark 6).
2 Rub the insides of each mackerel with lemon juice and season with freshly ground black pepper.

3 Mix the mushrooms with the parsley and stuff the cavity of each mackerel with the mixture.
4 Wrap each fish in foil and put the parcels on a baking sheet. Bake at the top of the oven for 20 minutes. Serve hot, still in the foil.

Smoked Mackerel and Courgette (Zucchini) Risotto

Smoked mackerel has such a strong flavour that a little goes a long way in a main-course dish like this. Sweetcorn kernels could be used in place of the courgettes (zucchini) as could lightly cooked broad (fava) beans.

Supplies 9g fat and 340 calories per portion.

Imperial/metric	Serves 5	American
4 oz (100g)	onion, finely chopped	⅔ cup
1 tsp	olive oil	1 tsp
10 oz (280g)	long grain Italian brown rice	1¼ cups
15 fl oz (450ml)	water	2 cups
12 oz (375g)	courgettes/zucchini, cut into 1-in pieces and quartered lengthwise	11 cups
¼ tsp	mixed herbs	¼ tsp
1 large	red pepper/sweet red pepper, deseeded and chopped	1 large
10 oz (280g)	smoked mackerel fillet, skinned and flaked freshly ground black pepper	10 oz

1 Put the onion in a pan with the olive oil and heat gently.
2 Stir in the rice, coat the grains with oil.
3 Add the water, courgettes (zucchini) and herbs, cover, bring to the boil, then simmer for 10 minutes.
4 Add the pepper (sweet pepper) and simmer for 10–15 minutes more until the rice is tender and the fluid has been absorbed.
5 Turn off the heat, flake in the smoked mackerel, season to taste with freshly ground black pepper and let the rice stand for a few minutes to let the flavours mingle. Serve either hot on its own or cool with a side salad.

Lemony Drumsticks

Chicken drumsticks are a useful addition to packed lunch-boxes and picnics. This recipe is fast and easy.

Supplies 5g fat and 150 calories per portion.

Imperial/metric	Serves 4	American
4	chicken drumsticks	4
1	lemon, juice of	1
½ tsp	dried thyme	½ tsp
	freshly ground black pepper	

1 Wipe the drumsticks.
2 In a small bowl, mix together the lemon juice, thyme and freshly ground black pepper.
3 Arrange the drumsticks on a barbecue or grill (broiler) pan and brush the lemon juice mixture over them.

4 Cook the chicken for 5 minutes. Turn and baste with the lemon mixture
5 Cook for a further 5 minutes, baste again and finish off for 2 more minutes. Serve either hot or cold.

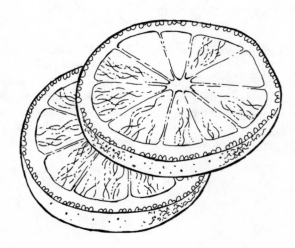

Chestnut Roast

An ideal vegetarian alternative to Christmas dinner, chestnuts are lower in fat than many nuts. Dried chestnuts, available from some health food stores, need to be soaked overnight before cooking, but they eliminate the lengthy shelling process involved when using fresh chestnuts.

Supplies 2.7g fat and 220 calories per portion.

Imperial/metric	Serves 5	American
10 oz (250g)	chestnuts, dried, soaked overnight	10 oz
3	celery sticks/stalks, finely chopped	3
2	cloves garlic, crushed/minced	2
6 oz (175g)	onion, finely chopped	1 cup
6 oz (175g)	carrots, scrubbed and finely grated	1 cup
1	lemon, grated rind of	1
3 tbs	fresh parsley, chopped	3 tbs
1½ tsp	dried thyme	1½ tsp
1 lb (450g)	Brussels sprouts	1 lb
	skimmed milk to mix	
¼ pt (150ml)	vegetable stock	⅔ cup
	freshly ground black pepper	

1 Drain the chestnuts. Put them in a pan with cold water and cover. Simmer for approximately 50 minutes until soft. Alternatively, pressure cook for 20 minutes at 15 lb (6 kilos) pressure.
2 While the chestnuts are cooking, mix together the celery, garlic, onion and carrots in a bowl with the lemon rind, parsley and thyme.
3 Preheat the oven to 375°F/190°C (Gas Mark 5). Prepare the Brussels sprouts and cook until tender. Drain and chop them finely. Season and mix with a little skimmed milk to make a smooth purée.

4 When the chestnuts are cooked, drain and chop them finely and mix in with the celery, garlic, onion and carrots. Mix in well with the hands as this helps to purée the chestnuts.
5 Add the stock and season with freshly ground black pepper. Have ready a greased 2-lb (700g) loaf tin (pan). Put half the chestnut mixture in the pan, add the sprout purée and then top with the remaining chestnut mixture. Cover with foil and bake in the preheated oven for 45 minutes. Serve hot or cold.

Mushroom-stuffed Marrow Rings

Supplies 7g fat and 160 calories per portion.

Imperial/metric	Serves 4	American
1 medium	marrow/squash	1 medium
2 oz (50g)	onion, finely chopped	⅓ cup
2 oz (50g)	carrot, finely grated	⅓ cup
1	celery stick/stalk, finely chopped	1
4 oz (100g)	button mushrooms, finely chopped	1½ cups
2	frozen cubes vegetable stock	2
4 oz (100g)	fresh wholemeal/whole wheat breadcrumbs	2 cups
2 oz (50g)	hazelnuts, ground	⅓ cup
½ tsp dried	sage	½ tsp dried
or 1 tsp fresh		*or* 1 tsp fresh
½ tsp dried	thyme	½ tsp dried
or 1 tsp fresh		*or* 1 tsp fresh
	freshly ground black pepper	
¼ pt (150ml)	vegetable stock	⅔ cup
2 tbs	sesame seeds	2 tbs
3 tbs	cold water	3 tbs

1 Preheat the oven to 400°F/200°C (Gas Mark 6).

2 Cut the marrow (squash) into slices ¾ in (2cm) thick. Scoop out the seeds. Steam or plunge into boiling water and cook for 5–8 minutes until just tender. Drain.

3 Sauté the onion, carrot, celery and mushrooms together over a low heat in the stock cubes, for a few minutes.

4 Tip the vegetables into a mixing bowl and stir in the breadcrumbs, ground hazelnuts, sage, thyme and a little freshly ground black pepper. Bind together with the stock.

5 Put the marrow (squash) rings, in a shallow ovenproof dish. Divide the mixture between the marrow (squash) rings, pressing it into the centres firmly. Scatter sesame seeds on top. Spoon 3 tbs cold water into the bottom of the dish and cover with aluminium foil.

6 Bake in the centre of the preheated oven for 30 minutes. Serve at once.

Rich Vegetable Sauce

*A meatless answer to Bolognese sauce. The addition of sunflower oil helps
to boost the flavour.*

Supplies 2.6g fat and 80 calories per portion.

Imperial/metric	Serves 4	American
2	cloves garlic, crushed/minced	2
½ lb (225g)	onion, finely chopped	1⅓ cups
2	celery sticks/stalks, finely chopped	2
½ lb (225g)	carrot, scrubbed and finely diced	1⅓ cups
2 tsp	sunflower oil	2 tsp
1	frozen cube vegetable stock	1
1 lb (450g) fresh	tomatoes	1 lb fresh
or 14-oz (397g) tin		*or* 14-oz can
¼ pt (150ml)	tomato purée/paste	⅔ cup
2 tsp	fresh oregano	2 tsp
½ lb (225g)	button mushrooms, sliced	3 cups
1	green pepper/sweet green pepper, deseeded and chopped	1
	freshly ground black pepper	

1 Cook the garlic, onion, celery and carrots gently in the sunflower oil and frozen stock for 2 minutes.
2 Add the tomatoes (skinned if fresh), vegetable stock, tomato purée (paste), oregano and mushrooms and cook for 20 minutes.
3 Add the pepper (sweet pepper) and continue to cook for a further 10 minutes. Season with freshly ground black pepper to taste and serve over spaghetti.

Chicken Liver Sauce

Chicken livers make a rich-tasting sauce that is also economical.

Supplies 7.4g fat and 200 calories per portion.

Imperial/metric	Serves 4	American
2	cloves garlic, crushed/minced	2
½ lb (225g)	onion, finely chopped	1⅓ cups
2	celery sticks/stalks, finely chopped	2
1 lb (450g)	chicken livers, trimmed and finely diced	1 lb
1 tbs	olive oil	1 tbs
6 oz (175g)	button mushrooms	3 cups
1 lb (450g) fresh	tomatoes	1 lb fresh
or 14-oz (397g) tin		*or* 14-oz can
¼ pt (150ml)	chicken stock	⅔ cup
¼ tsp	dried thyme	¼ tsp
¼ tsp	dried marjoram	¼ tsp
1	bay leaf	1
½ lb (225g)	carrot, scrubbed and finely grated	1⅓ cups
	freshly ground black pepper	

1 Sauté the garlic, onion, celery and chicken livers together in the olive oil for a few minutes until the chicken livers turn brown.
2 Add the mushrooms, tomatoes (skinned if fresh), chicken stock, thyme, marjoram and bay leaf. Bring to the boil, cover, reduce the heat and simmer for 25 minutes.
3 Add the carrots to the pan. Continue cooking for a further 5 minutes. Season with freshly ground black pepper and serve.

Mushroom and Pepper Sauce

Supplies 1.6g fat and 52 calories.

Imperial/metric	Serves 4	American
½ lb (225g)	onion, finely chopped	1⅓ cups
2	cloves garlic, crushed/minced	2
1 tsp	olive oil	1 tsp
1	frozen cube vegetable stock	1
¾ lb (325g)	field/open mushrooms, sliced	6 cups
1 lb (450g) fresh	tomatoes	1 lb fresh
or 14-oz (397g) tin		*or* 14-oz can
1 large *or* 2 small	red pepper/sweet red pepper	1 large *or* 2 small
1 tsp dried	basil	1 tsp dried
or 2 tsp fresh		*or* 2 tsp fresh
	freshly ground black pepper	

1 Sauté the onion and the garlic together in the olive oil and stock for 3 minutes.
2 Add the mushrooms and tomatoes (skinned if using fresh). Deseed and cut the pepper (sweet pepper) into fine strips and add, too.

3 Add the remaining ingredients to the sauce and bring to the boil. Reduce the heat and simmer for 40 minutes. Season to taste with freshly ground black pepper before serving.

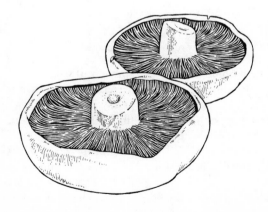

Spinach and Soft Cheese Lasagne

A classic vegetarian alternative to standard lasagne — just as popular with meat-eaters, too.

Supplies 5.8g fat and 320 calories per portion.

Imperial/metric	Serves 4	American
½ lb (225g)	wholemeal/whole wheat lasagne	½ lb
	For the sauce:	
1	clove garlic, crushed/minced	1
4 oz (100g)	onion, chopped	⅔ cup
1 small	red pepper/sweet red pepper, deseeded and chopped	1 small
1 tsp	olive oil	1 tsp
1 lb (450g)	tomatoes	1 lb fresh
or 14-oz (397g) tin		*or* 14-oz can
¾ tsp dried	basil	¾ tsp dried
or 1½ tsp fresh	basil	*or* 1½ tsp fresh
	freshly ground black pepper	
	For the filling:	
¾ lb (325g)	spinach	7½ cups fresh
		or 1½ cups defrosted
½ lb (225g)	low-fat soft cheese	½ lb
pinch	nutmeg	pinch
	parsley, chopped, to garnish	

1 Plunge the lasagne into a pan of boiling water and bring to the boil. Cook for 10 minutes until *al dente*, almost soft, then drain.
2 Sauté the garlic, onion and pepper (sweet pepper) gently in the olive oil. Add the tomatoes (skinned if fresh) and basil. Simmer for 20 minutes. Season to taste with freshly ground black pepper.
3 While the sauce is cooking, prepare the spinach. If using fresh, wash it thoroughly, chop it roughly and put it in a pan of water. Cook it gently for 4 minutes, drain and then chop it finely. If using frozen, defrost it, heat it, then chop it finely.
4 Mix the spinach with the low-fat soft cheese and add the nutmeg.
5 Preheat the oven to 375°F/190°C (Gas Mark 5). Put a layer of lasagne in the bottom of a lightly

greased ovenproof baking dish. Add a layer of the tomato sauce, then lasagne, then spinach and finally top with tomato sauce. Cover with foil and bake for 30 minutes in the centre of the oven. Sprinkle chopped parsley on the top before serving.

Savoury Bean Ring

Baking this mixture in a ring tin (tube pan) gives a convenient centre for filling with a salad. Alternatively, bake it in a loaf tin (pan) or shape into burgers and bake in the oven.

Supplies 1.9g fat and 240g calories each.

Imperial/metric	Serves 4	American
6 oz (175g)	butter/lima beans, soaked overnight	1 cup
6 oz (175g)	fresh wholemeal/whole wheat breadcrumbs	3 cups
2	celery sticks/stalks, finely chopped	2
4 oz (100g)	onion, finely chopped	⅔ cup
6 oz (175g)	mushrooms, finely chopped	3 cups
6 oz (175g)	carrot, scrubbed and finely grated	1 cup
2 tbs	tomato purée/paste	2 tbs
3 tbs	vegetable stock	3 tbs
	few drops of *Tabasco* sauce	
½ tsp	dried marjoram	½ tsp
¼ tsp	dried thyme	¼ tsp
	freshly ground black pepper	

1 Drain the beans. Put them in a pan and cover with water. Cook for 1¾–2 hours until really soft. Alternatively, pressure cook them at 15 lb (6 kilos) pressure for 20 minutes.
2 Preheat the oven to 375°F/190°C (Gas Mark 5).
3 When the beans are cooked, drain and mash them to a purée. Stir in the breadcrumbs.
4 Stir the celery, onion, mushrooms and carrot into the bean mixture.

5 Add the tomato purée (paste), stock, *Tabasco* sauce, marjoram, thyme and a little freshly ground black pepper and mix to a smooth consistency, adding a little extra stock if the mixture is a little dry.
6 Lightly oil a ring tin (tube pan) and press the mixture down well inside. Cover with foil and bake in the oven for 35 minutes. Turn it out (unmold) carefully and fill the centre with a salad.

Shepherdess Pie

The basic mixture of lentils with vegetables can be used in many dishes.
Try it as a topping for wholemeal (whole wheat) spaghetti, stir in cooked
brown rice for a tasty risotto or use it to stuff peppers (sweet peppers). Here
it is topped with mashed potatoes to make a vegetarian, low-fat and
economical version of a family favourite.

Supplies 1.8g fat and 270 calories per portion.

Imperial/metric	Serves 6	American
6 oz (175g)	onion, finely chopped	1 cup
1	clove garlic, crushed/minced	1
6 oz (175g)	carrot, scrubbed and finely diced	1 cup
2	celery sticks/stalks, finely diced	2
1 tsp	olive oil	1 tsp
3	frozen cubes of stock	3
6 oz (175g)	mushrooms, chopped	2¼ cups
1	green pepper/sweet green pepper, deseeded and chopped	1
10 oz (275g)	brown lentils	1½ cups
2×14-oz (397g) tins	tomatoes	2×14-oz cans
¼ pt (150ml)	vegetable stock	⅔ cup
2	bay leaves	2
1 tsp	dried marjoram	1 tsp
	freshly ground black pepper	
	For the topping:	
1½ lb (675g)	potatoes	4 cups
	bay leaf *or* sprig of mint	
	skimmed milk (to mix with potatoes)	
	freshly ground black pepper	

1 Put the onion, garlic, carrots, celery, olive oil and frozen stock cubes in a pan and cook for 2 minutes.
2 Stir in the mushrooms, pepper (sweet pepper), lentils, tomatoes, vegetable stock, bay leaves and marjoram. Cover, bring to the boil, then turn down the heat and let the mixture simmer for 40 minutes.

3 After the lentils have been cooking for 20 minutes, peel the potatoes and cut into pieces 1½ in (4cm) across. Put them in a pan with cold water and either the bay leaf or the mint. Bring to the boil, then reduce the heat and cook for 20–25 minutes until soft. Drain at once, remove the herbs, mash with milk until smooth and season to taste with freshly ground black pepper.

4 Heat the grill (broiler) to very hot. Put the lentil mixture into a heatproof dish and top with the potato. Cook under the grill (broiler) for 5–7 minutes until the top turns a crispy golden brown. Serve hot with a green vegetable.

Butter (Lima) Bean Goulash

Supplies 0.8g fat and 230 calories each.

Imperial/metric	Serves 4	American
4 oz (100g)	onion, finely chopped	⅔ cup
2	celery sticks/stalks, finely chopped	2
½ lb (225g)	carrot, scrubbed and thinly sliced	1⅓ cups
1	green pepper/sweet green pepper, deseeded and sliced	1
1	red pepper/sweet red pepper, deseeded and sliced	1
4 tbs	sweetcorn kernels	4 tbs
½ lb (225g)	butter/lima beans, soaked overnight	1⅓ cups
1 pt (600ml)	vegetable stock	2½ cups
14-oz (397-g) tin	tomatoes	14-oz can
small tin	tomato purée/paste	small can
2	bay leaves	2
1 tbs	paprika	1 tbs
¼ tsp	oregano	¼ tsp
	freshly ground black pepper	
	parsley, chopped, to garnish	

1 Preheat the oven to 375°F/190°C (Gas Mark 5). Put the onion, celery, carrot, peppers (sweet peppers), sweetcorn and drained butter beans in a casserole dish and pour the vegetable stock and tomatoes over them.

2 Stir in the tomato purée (paste), bay leaves, paprika and oregano.

3 Cover and bake in the centre of the oven for 1½–2 hours until the beans are just tender. Season to taste with freshly ground black pepper and serve garnished with the parsley.

Boston Beans

A home-made alternative to canned beans.

Supplies 2g fat and 200 calories each.

Imperial/metric	Serves 4	American
½ lb (225g)	haricot/navy beans, soaked overnight	1 cup
1	onion, finely chopped	1
1 tsp	sunflower oil	1 tsp
1 tbs	molasses	1 tbs
1 tsp	mustard	1 tsp
14-oz (397-g) tin	tomatoes	14-oz can
¼ pt (150ml)	vegetable stock	⅔ cup
1 tbs	tomato purée/paste	1 tbs
	freshly ground black pepper	

1 Drain the beans. Put them in a pan and cover with cold water. Bring to the boil and cook them for 20 minutes. Drain.

2 Sauté the onion gently in the sunflower oil for 2 minutes. Stir in the molasses, mustard, tomatoes, vegetable stock, tomato purée (paste) and drained beans.

3 Bring to the boil, then reduce and simmer gently for 40–45 minutes until the beans are tender. Season to taste with freshly ground black pepper and serve.

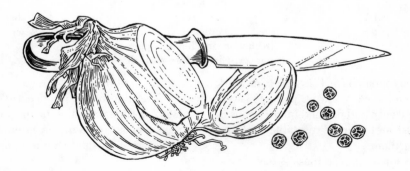

Bean and Leek Braise

Black-eye beans are useful because they do not need soaking before cooking. They will cook in about 45–50 minutes.

Supplies 0.7g fat and 160 calories per portion.

Imperial/metric	Serves 4	American
½ lb (225g)	leeks	2 cups
6 oz (175g)	carrot, scrubbed and thinly sliced	1 cup
6 oz (175g)	swede/rutabaga, peeled and diced	1 cup
1	eating/dessert apple, cored and diced	1
6 oz (175g)	black-eye beans	⅔ cup
1 pt (600ml)	vegetable stock	2½ cups
½ tsp	yeast extract	½ tsp
1 tsp fresh	sage	1 tsp fresh
or ½ tsp dried		*or* ½ tsp dried
1	bay leaf	1
	freshly ground black pepper	

1 Preheat the oven to 375°F/190°C (Gas Mark 5).

2 Cut the leeks into ½-in (1-cm) thick slices.

3 Put the leeks, carrot, swede (rutabaga) and apple in a casserole dish and add the beans, stock, yeast extract, sage and bay leaf.

4 Cover, place in the preheated oven and bake' for 50 minutes (check that the mixture does not become too dry and add extra stock if needed). Season to taste with freshly ground black pepper and serve.

Winter Barley Hot Pot

Unpolished pearl (pot) barley is more nutritious than pearl (pot) barley, which has been refined. Health food stores sell unpolished pearl (pot) barley — it's cheap, filling and ideal for warming winter stews like this one.

Supplies 0.4g fat and 160 calories per portion.

Imperial/metric	Serves 4	American
4 oz (100g)	onion, finely chopped	⅔ cup
½ lb (225g)	carrots, scrubbed and sliced	1⅓ cups
½ lb (225g)	swede/rutabaga, peeled and diced	1⅓ cups
½ lb (225g)	parsnip, scrubbed and diced	1⅓ cups
1	celery stick/stalk, finely chopped	1
4 oz (100g)	unpolished pearl/pot barley	½ cup
1½ pt (900ml)	vegetable stock	3¾ cups
1 tsp	yeast extract	1 tsp
1 tbs	tomato purée/paste	1 tbs
pinch	dried thyme	pinch
1	bay leaf	1
pinch	marjoram	pinch
	freshly ground black pepper	

1 Preheat the oven to 375°F/190°C (Gas Mark 5).

2 Put all the vegetables in a large casserole dish, add the barley, pour the stock over, stir in the yeast extract, tomato purée (paste), thyme, bay leaf and marjoram. Cover and bake at the top of the preheated oven for 1½ hours. Season to taste with freshly ground black pepper and serve.

Savoury Buckwheat

You can use buckwheat in place of rice. Simply cook it in good stock and with some vegetables to add flavour. Cauliflower florets seem to complement this grain well.

Supplies 1.6g fat and 240 calories per portion.

Imperial/metric	Serves 4	American
2	celery sticks/stalks, finely chopped	2
4 oz (100g)	onion, finely chopped	⅔ cup
1 tsp	sunflower oil	1 tsp
2	frozen cubes of stock	2
½ lb (225g)	buckwheat	½ cup
1 small	cauliflower, broken into florets	1 small
2	bay leaves	2
18 fl oz (540ml)	vegetable stock	2⅓ cups
2 tsp fresh	sage	2 tsp fresh
or 1 tsp dried		*or* 1 tsp dried
½ lb (225g)	carrot, finely grated	1⅓ cups
	freshly ground black pepper	

1 Cook the celery and onion gently in the sunflower oil and frozen stock for 3 minutes.
2 Stir in the buckwheat, cauliflower florets, bay leaves, vegetable stock and the sage (if using dried).
3 Bring to the boil, cover and reduce the heat. Simmer for 20 minutes until the liquid is absorbed and the buckwheat is soft.
4 Stir in the carrot and sage, if using fresh, and season with freshly ground black pepper. Turn off the heat but leave the pan on the cooker to stand for 5 minutes before serving.

Sunflower Crunch Risotto

Toast the sunflower seeds first to bring out their nutty flavour.

Supplies 9.8g fat and 240 calories.

Imperial/metric	Serves 4	American
2	frozen cubes of stock	2
4 oz (100g)	onion, finely chopped	⅔ cup
1	celery stick/stalk, finely chopped	1
½ tsp dried	thyme	½ tsp dried
or 1 tsp fresh		*or* 1 tsp fresh
½ lb (225g)	long grain brown rice	1 cup
1 pt (600ml)	vegetable stock	2½ cups
1	bay leaf	1
1 small	cauliflower, broken into small florets	1 small
4 oz (100g)	courgettes/zucchini, sliced, *or*	2 cups
	button mushrooms *or* sweetcorn kernels	
3 oz (75g)	sunflower seeds	generous ½ cup
4 oz (100g)	carrots, finely grated	⅔ cup
	freshly ground black pepper	

1 Melt the frozen stock cubes in a large pan. Add the onion, celery and thyme and simmer for 1 minute. Stir in the rice and simmer for 1 minute.

2 Add the rest of the stock and the bay leaf. Bring to the boil, add the cauliflower florets and cover. Simmer for 15 minutes.

3 Lift the lid and, without disturbing the mixture, add the sliced courgettes (zucchini), mushrooms or sweetcorn kernels and cook for a further 10 minutes (if the mixture looks a touch dry add a little more stock).

4 Meanwhile, toast the sunflower seeds, either by heating a grill (broiler) and putting the seeds in the bottom of the pan and toasting until just golden, or heat up a heavy-based frying pan (skillet) (without fat) and heat the seeds until golden.

5 Check that the rice is cooked — it should be just tender without being stodgy. Add the grated carrots and sunflower seeds and season with freshly ground black pepper. If there is any surplus liquid in the bottom of the pan turn up the heat and let it boil away. Serve hot.

Walnut and Rice Bake

Supplies 11g fat and 280 calories per portion.

Imperial/metric	Serves 5	American
6 oz (175g)	long grain brown rice	¾ cup
4 oz (100g)	walnuts/English walnuts	¾ cup
6 oz (175g)	carrot, scrubbed and finely grated	1 cup
4 oz (100g)	onion, finely chopped	⅔ cup
2 small *or* 1 large	red pepper/sweet red pepper	2 small *or* 1 large
1 tsp	dried thyme	1 tsp
4 tbs	sweetcorn kernels *or* celery stick/stalk, finely chopped	4 tbs
4 tbs	tomato purée (paste)	4 tbs
1	free-range egg, beaten	1
4 tbs	vegetable stock	4 tbs

1 Put the rice into a pan with cold water, bring to the boil, reduce the heat and simmer for 25–30 minutes until just tender. Drain and set aside.

2 Preheat the oven to 400°F/200°C (Gas Mark 6).

3 Put the walnuts (English walnuts) in a blender and grind.

4 Mix the walnuts (English walnuts), carrot, onion and pepper (sweet pepper) together in a bowl, blending thoroughly and evenly. Add the thyme and the sweetcorn or celery and bind with the tomato purée (paste), beaten egg and vegetable stock.

5 Lightly grease a 2 lb (900g) loaf tin (pan) and line the bottom with greaseproof (waxed) paper. Pour in the mixture and press it down firmly.

6 Cover with foil and bake in the preheated oven for 35–40 minutes, removing the foil for the last five minutes. Serve in slices either hot or cold with a crisp side salad.

Cauliflower with Cumin and Coriander

Supplies 1.2g fat and 55 calories per portion.

Imperial/metric	Serves 4	American
2	onions, finely chopped	2
2	cloves garlic, crushed/minced	2
⅜-in (1-cm) cube	root ginger, peeled and grated	½-in cube
4 tbs	cold water	4 tbs
1 tsp	sunflower oil	1 tsp
½ tsp	cumin seeds	½ tsp
3	tomatoes, chopped	3
½ tsp	ground cumin	½ tsp
1 tsp	ground coriander	1 tsp
¼ tsp	turmeric	¼ tsp
1 large	cauliflower, broken into florets	1 large
1 tsp	garam masala	1 tsp

1 Put half the chopped onion in the goblet of a liquidizer (blender) with the garlic, ginger and water and blend to a purée.

2 Heat the sunflower oil and onion, garlic and ginger paste in a large saucepan and add the cumin seeds. Cook for 1 minute, then add the remaining onion and cook for 1 more minute.

3 Stir in the tomatoes, ground cumin, ground coriander and turmeric and cook for 4 minutes over a low heat.

4 Add the cauliflower florets and stir in well. Add a further tbs of water and cover. Simmer gently for 20 minutes.

5 Turn off the heat and add the garam masala. Leave to stand on the hot plate for 5 minutes before serving.

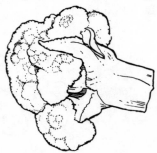

Prawn (Large Shrimp) and Courgette (Zucchini) Curry

Quick to prepare, this curry can be made with less chilli if you prefer a milder-tasting dish.

Supplies 4g fat and 250 calories per portion.

Imperial/metric	Serves 4	American
1 lb (450g)	courgettes/zucchini	1 lb
4 oz (100g)	onion, chopped	⅔ cup
4	cloves garlic, chopped	4
½-in (1cm) cube	root ginger, peeled and grated	½-in cube
5 tbs	water	5 tbs
2 tsp	sunflower or sesame oil	2 tsp
1 tsp	cumin seeds	1 tsp
1 tsp	ground coriander	1 tsp
1 tsp	ground cumin	1 tsp
1	green chilli/green chili pepper, deseeded and chopped	1
3	canned tomatoes	3
2 tbs	tomato juice from can	2 tbs
1 lb (450g)	prawns/large shrimp, peeled	1 lb
1 tsp	lemon juice	1 tsp
	freshly ground black pepper	

1 Wipe the courgettes (zucchini) and cut into fine sticks, 1-in (2.5-cm) long.
2 Put the onion, garlic and ginger, together with the water, in the goblet of a liquidizer (blender) and blend until smooth.
3 Heat the oil in a frying pan (skillet) and add the cumin seeds. Let them sizzle and then pour in the onion, garlic and ginger paste. Cook for 1 minute then add the ground coriander, ground cumin, chilli (chili pepper) and cayenne pepper and cook for 2 minutes.
4 Now add the tomatoes and juice and stir in the courgettes (zucchini) sticks. Cook for 5 minutes.
5 Stir in the prawns (large shrimp) and lemon juice and cook for a further 2 minutes. Season to taste with freshly ground black pepper and serve at once, with plain boiled or spiced rice, with mushrooms (see page 77).

Black-eye Beans with Mushrooms

Supplies 1g fat and 145 calories each.

Imperial/metric	Serves 4	American
½ lb (225g)	black-eye beans	1 cup
1 small	onion, chopped	1 small
1	green chilli/green chili pepper, chopped	1
½-in (1-cm) piece	root ginger, grated	½-in piece
6	black peppercorns	6
½-in (1-cm) piece	cinnamon stick	½-in piece
2	cloves garlic, crushed/minced	2
2	frozen cubes vegetable stock	2
1 tsp	ground coriander	1 tsp
½ tsp	ground cumin	½ tsp
½ tsp	turmeric	½ tsp
1 tsp	garam masala	1 tsp
1 tsp	fresh lemon juice	1 tsp
6 oz (175g)	button mushrooms	3 cups
	freshly ground black pepper	

1 Put the beans in a pan with the onion, chilli (chili pepper), ginger, peppercorns and cinnamon. Cover with water, bring to the boil, cover the pan and simmer for 20 minutes. Drain, reserving the cooking liquid.

2 Sauté the garlic in the stock for 2 minutes, then stir in the spices. Cook for 1 minute. Now add the lemon juice and mushrooms, drained beans and about ½-¾ pt (285-425ml/1⅓-2 cups) stock reserved from beans (enough to make a sauce).

3 Simmer for a further 20 minutes until the beans are tender. Serve at once.

Spiced Rice

*This dish can be varied in many ways by adding different vegetables —
chopped mushrooms, cauliflower florets, diced red and green pepper (red
and green sweet pepper), a few cooked peas. This makes an excellent
accompaniment to curried dishes.*

Supplies under 1g fat and 225 calories per portion.

Imperial/metric	Serves 4	American
4 oz (100g)	onion, finely chopped	⅔ cup
1	celery stick/stalk, finely chopped	1
1	clove garlic, crushed/minced	1
6 oz (175g)	carrot, scrubbed and diced	1 cup
3	frozen cubes vegetable stock	3
½ tsp	ground coriander	½ tsp
½ tsp	ground cumin	½ tsp
¼ tsp	turmeric	¼ tsp
pinch	cayenne pepper	pinch
½ lb (225g)	long grain brown rice	1 cup
18 fl oz (540ml)	vegetable stock	2⅓ cups
	freshly ground black pepper	
	fresh coriander to garnish	

1 Sauté the onion, celery, garlic and carrot together in the melted stock cubes for 2 minutes.
2 Stir in the coriander, cumin, turmeric and cayenne pepper and cook for 1 minute. Now add the rice and stir so that the grains are coated with the spice mixture.
3 Pour in the stock. Bring to the boil then cover, reduce the heat and let it simmer for 30 minutes.
4 Remove the lid, and see if the rice is ready. If too much liquid remains, turn up the heat and leave the lid off to let it evaporate. Season to taste with freshly ground black pepper and garnish with fresh coriander. Serve hot.

Potato-topped Pie

*Conventional pastry is very high in fat. This recipe combines mashed
potato with wholemeal (whole wheat) flour to give a tasty topping.*

Supplies under 1g fat and 160 calories per portion.

Imperial/metric	Serves 4	American
	For the topping:	
6 oz (175g)	potatoes, peeled and cut into 2-in (5-cm) cubes	1 cup
	skimmed milk to mash	
	freshly ground black pepper	
4 oz (100g)	wholemeal/whole wheat flour	1 cup
	For the filling:	
½ pt (300ml)	vegetable stock	1⅓ cups
1 small	onion, chopped	1 small
1	celery stick/stalk, chopped	1
1	clove garlic, crushed/minced	1
4 oz (100g)	carrot, scrubbed and sliced	⅔ cup
6 oz (150g)	swede/rutabaga, peeled and finely diced	1 cup
6 oz (150g)	parsnip, peeled and finely diced	1 cup
½ tsp dried	sage	½ tsp dried
or 1 tsp fresh		*or* 1 tsp fresh
4 oz (100g)	button mushrooms, chopped	1½ cups
	freshly ground black pepper	

1 Cover the potatoes with cold water, bring to the boil then reduce the heat and cook for 20 minutes or until soft. Drain and mash with a little skimmed milk. Season to taste with freshly ground black pepper and stir in the wholemeal (whole wheat) flour leave to cool.

2 Preheat the oven to 400°F/200°C (Gas Mark 6).

3 Meanwhile, prepare the filling. Heat 2 tablespoons of the stock in a pan and stir in the onion, celery and garlic. Cook for 2 minutes. Add the carrot, swede/rutabaga and parsnip and cook for a further minute. Now add the remaining stock and the sage and cook for 10 minutes. Stir in the mushrooms and season to taste with freshly ground black pepper. Pour into a deep pie dish.

4 Roll out the potato mixture on a lightly floured surface. Carefully lower over filling, trim and brush with a little skimmed milk. Make a few air vents to let steam escape. Bake in the preheated oven for 15 minutes, then lower the heat to 350°F/180°C (Gas Mark 4) for 10–15 minutes to finish cooking.

Chapter 6

Vegetable Dishes

Vegetables and fruits are vital ingredients in a healthy diet. Without them, we would receive no vitamin C and without this vitamin our bodies would begin to deteriorate due to the deficiency disease scurvy. So daily servings of both fruits and vegetables are essential but so too is care in cooking. Vitamin C is one of the most fragile nutrients, easily destroyed by heat and by exposure to the air once the fruits or vegetables are cut. In order to make the most of the vitamin naturally present in vegetables and fruits, take care to follow these basic golden rules:

● prepare as close to serving as possible

● eat raw or cook quickly and lightly

● cook either by steaming over fast boiling water or plunge into a small amount of water that is already boiling

● eat as soon as produce is cooked (keeping food hot destroys vitamin C)

● cut with a sharp knife rather than a blunt one to cause less cell disruption.

Many ways of serving vegetables simply add extra fat. Be wary of smothering cooked vegetables with butter and avoid cooking methods like roasting and frying, which depend on large amounts of fat for success. Instead, simply boil produce or steam and make sure that the main course of your meal has a tasty sauce or dresssing to liven up the vegetables. Alternatively, look at some of the recipes in this chapter that add natural flavourings to vegetables to produce more interesting cooked side dishes. Serve vegetables as salads with low-fat salad dressings made with yogurt, lemon juice, vinegar and less oil than usual.

Carrot and Chervil Salad

Supplies less than 1g fat and 30 calories per portion.

Imperial/metric	Serves 4	American
¾ lb (325g)	carrots, scrubbed and coarsely grated	2 cups
1 tsp fresh	chervil	1 tsp fresh
or ½ tsp dried		*or* ½ tsp dried
	freshly ground black pepper	
1	green pepper/sweet green pepper, deseeded and finely chopped	1
3 tbs	natural/unsweetened yogurt	3 tbs

1 Put the carrots in a bowl with the chervil and season with freshly ground black pepper.
2 Add the pepper (sweet pepper) to the bowl with the natural yogurt. Toss together until thoroughly mixed and serve.

Creamy Carrot Purée

This combination of carrots and swede (rutabaga) is a favourite. Use skimmed milk rather than full fat milk and butter to work the cooked vegetables to a soft purée. Season generously.

Supplies only a trace of fat and 70 calories per portion.

Imperial/metric	Serves 4	American
2 lb (900g)	swede/rutabaga, peeled and roughly diced	5⅓ cups
¾ lb (325g)	carrots, scrubbed and chopped	2 cups
1	bay leaf	1
	skimmed milk to mix	
	freshly ground black pepper	

1 Put the swede (rutabaga) and carrot in a large pan and add enough water to come halfway up the pan and add the bay leaf. Cover, bring to the boil, then reduce the heat and simmer for 40 minutes, or until both the carrot and swede are really soft.

2 Drain the vegetables and remove the bay leaf. Mash with enough milk to give a soft purée. Season generously with freshly ground black pepper. Reheat gently and serve.

Braised Celery

Celery is a popular ingredient in crunchy salads, but the vegetable is also good served hot. This recipe mixes carrots with celery and a good stock.

Supplies only a trace of fat and 70 calories per portion.

Imperial/metric	Serves 4	American
head	celery	head
¾ lb (325g)	carrots	¾ lb
1	bay leaf	1
¾ pt (450ml)	vegetable stock	2 cups
	freshly ground black pepper	

1 Preheat the oven to 400°F/200°C (Gas Mark 6).

2 Scrub the celery and cut into 3-in (7.5-cm) lengths.

3 Scrub the carrots and cut into long strips.

4 Put the celery and carrot into a casserole dish with the bay leaf and stock. Cover tightly and bake for 30 minutes in the centre of the preheated oven. Season to taste with freshly ground black pepper and serve at once.

Low-fat Ratatouille

Use less olive oil than you would usually, making up the difference with well-flavoured vegetable stock. This recipe freezes well so is a good way of using up a glut of courgettes (zucchini) from the garden.

Supplies 1.3g fat and 70 calories per portion.

Imperial/metric	Serves 4	American
½ lb (225g)	aubergine/eggplant	3¼ cups
6 oz (175g)	onion, finely chopped	1 cup
3	cloves garlic, crushed/minced	3
1 tsp	olive oil	1 tsp
2	frozen cubes stock	2
1 tsp dried	basil	1 tsp dried
or 2 tsp fresh		*or* 2 tsp fresh
14-oz (397-g) tin	tomatoes, skinned if fresh	14-oz can
or 1 lb fresh		*or* 1 lb fresh
¾ lb (325g)	courgettes/zucchini, sliced	5 cups
1 large	green pepper/sweet green pepper deseeded and chopped	1 large
4 oz (100g)	button mushrooms	2 cups
	freshly ground black pepper	

1 Dice the aubergine (eggplant) into ½-in (1-cm) cubes.

2 Cook the aubergine (eggplant) cubes, onion and garlic in the olive oil and frozen stock over a low heat for 5 minutes. Stir in the basil and cook for 1 minute more.

3 Add the tomatoes, courgettes (zucchini), green pepper (sweet green pepper) and mushrooms. Bring to the boil then reduce the heat and let it simmer gently for 30 minutes. Season with freshly ground black pepper and either serve hot or let it cool completely and serve chilled.

Courgette (Zucchini) and Tomato Salad

Supplies 4.5g fat and 60 calories per portion.

Imperial/metric	Serves 4	American
10 oz (275g)	courgettes/zucchini	4 cups
1	clove garlic, crushed/minced	1
1 tbs	olive oil	1 tbs
½	lemon, juice of	½
4	tomatoes, sliced	4
2 tbs	fresh parsley, chopped	2 tbs

1 Wipe the courgettes (zucchini) and cut into slices approximately ⅜ in (1cm) thick.
2 Steam lightly or plunge into boiling water and cook for 2 minutes. Drain and immediately toss in a bowl with the garlic, olive oil and lemon juice. Season to taste with freshly ground black pepper.
3 Add the tomatoes to the bowl with the parsley. Set aside to bring out the flavours before serving.

Cucumber Cooler

This refreshing salad goes particularly well with curries but can be served as a simple side salad with a variety of summer dishes, too.

Supplies less than 1g fat and 25 calories per portion.

Imperial/metric	Serves 4	American
4-in (10-cm) piece	cucumber, finely diced	4-in piece
4 oz (100g)	seedless white grapes, washed and halved	½ bunch
4 tbs	natural/unsweetened yogurt	4 tbs
2 tsp	chives, chopped	2 tsp
	freshly ground black pepper	

1 Mix the cucumber and grapes in a bowl.
2 Pour the yogurt over, add the chives and season to taste with freshly ground black pepper. Toss together thoroughly and chill before serving.

Spicy Mushrooms

An excellent accompaniment to Prawn (Large Shrimp) and Courgette (Zucchini) Curry (see page 75).

Supplies 1.6g fat and 100 calories each.

Imperial/metric	Serves 4	American
4	cloves garlic, crushed/minced	4
½-in (1-cm) cube	root ginger, peeled and grated	½-in cube
4 tbs	water	4 tbs
1 tsp	olive oil	1 tsp
¾ lb (325g)	button mushrooms, halved	6 cups
1 tsp	lemon juice	1 tsp
	freshly ground black pepper	

1 Put the garlic and ginger in the goblet of a liquidizer (blender) with the water and blend to a smooth paste.
2 Heat the olive oil in a saucepan and stir in the garlic and ginger paste. Heat for 1 minute then stir in the mushrooms. Lower the heat and simmer for 20 minutes, adding a little more water if needed.
3 Stir in the lemon juice, season to taste with freshly ground black pepper and serve.

Savoy Stir-fry

Savoy cabbage with its dark, crinkly leaves makes a good contrast to the beanshoots in this quick and easy dish.

Supplies only a trace of fat and 20 calories per portion.

Imperial/metric	*Serves 4*	American
4	frozen cubes stock	4
1 tbs	soy sauce	1 tbs
¾ lb (325g)	Savoy cabbage, finely shredded	3 cups
1 tsp	tomato purée/paste	1 tsp
2 handsful	beanshoots/beansprouts	2 handsful
2	spring onions/scallions, chopped	2
	freshly ground black pepper	

1 In a wok or large, heavy-based frying pan (skillet), heat the stock and soy sauce. Add the shredded cabbage and, stirring frequently, cook over a high heat for 3 minutes.

2 Stir in the tomato purée (paste) and beanshoots (beansprouts) and mix in thoroughly. Add the spring onions (scallions) and cook for a further 2–3 minutes. Season to taste with freshly ground black pepper and serve at once.

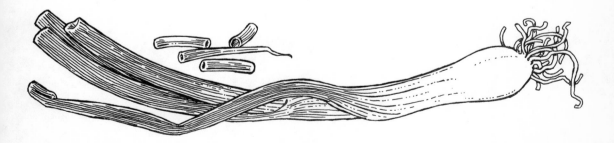

Red Cabbage Braise

A tangy way of serving red cabbage.

Supplies 1g fat and 80 calories per portion.

Imperial/metric	Serves 4	American
1 tsp	sunflower oil	1 tsp
2	frozen cubes vegetable stock	2
1 large	onion, finely chopped	1 large
1 medium	red cabbage, washed and finely shredded	1 medium
2	eating/dessert apples, chopped	2
1	green pepper/sweet green pepper, chopped	1
2 oz (50g)	sultanas/golden seedless raisins	⅓ cup
2 tbs	cider vinegar	2 tbs
1 tbs	vegetable stock or water	1 tbs
	freshly ground black pepper	

1 Heat the sunflower oil and stock in a pan and stir in the onion. Cook for 2 minutes.
2 Stir in the cabbage, apple and pepper (sweet pepper), sultanas (golden seedless raisins), vinegar and stock or water. Simmer for 35 minutes over a low heat then season to taste with freshly ground black pepper and serve at once.

Red Cabbage Crunch

Makes a colourful change from white cabbage in salads.

Supplies 1g fat and 50 calories per portion.

Imperial/metric	Serves 4	American
4	celery sticks/stalks, finely chopped	4
1	leek, trimmed and thinly sliced	1
2	sharp-tasting apples, cored and diced	2
1	lemon, juice of	1
½ lb (225g)	red cabbage, shredded	2 cups
2 oz (50g)	low-fat soft cheese	¼ cup
1 tbs	natural/unsweetened yogurt	1 tbs
½ tsp	dill seeds	½ tsp
	freshly ground black pepper	
1	green pepper/sweet green pepper, deseeded and sliced, to garnish	1

1 Mix the celery and leek together.
2 Mix the apples with the lemon juice to stop them browning.
3 Mix the red cabbage with the apple, then stir in the celery and leek mixture and toss together thoroughly.

4 Mix the soft cheese with the yogurt, dill seeds and freshly ground black pepper and pour over the salad. Toss thoroughly.
5 Garnish the salad with the pepper (sweet pepper) rings and serve.

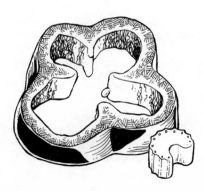

Potato and Onion Salad

Supplies less than 1g fat and 90 calories per portion.

Imperial/metric	Serves 4, as a side dish	American
¾ lb (325g)	potatoes	¾ lb
sprig	mint	sprig
4	spring onions/scallions, trimmed and chopped	4
¾-in (2-cm) piece	cucumber, finely diced	¾-in piece
4 tbs	natural/unsweetened yogurt	4 tbs
¼ tsp	dill seeds	¼ tsp
	freshly ground black pepper	

1 Scrub the potatoes and cut them into 2-in (5-cm) chunks. Put them into a pan with the mint and cover with cold water. Bring to the boil, then reduce the heat and simmer for 20 minutes or until the potatoes are just soft.
2 While the potatoes are cooking, mix the spring onions (scallions) and cucumber with the yogurt, dill seeds and freshly ground black pepper in a bowl.
3 When the potatoes are cooked, drain and dice them finely. Add them to the dressing and toss together thoroughly. Leave to cool before serving.

Watercress and Carrot Salad

Orange is a traditional accompaniment to watercress — here it is added as juice to give an unusual dressing.

Supplies 1g fat and 30 calories per portion.

Imperial/metric	Serves 4	American
bunch	watercress	bunch
½ lb (225g)	carrots, scrubbed and coarsely grated	1⅓ cups
1 tsp	sunflower oil	1 tsp
1 tbs	fresh orange juice	1 tbs
1	spring onion/scallion, chopped	1

1 Wash the watercress, trim off any yellow leaves and put them into a bowl.
2 Add the carrots to the watercress and mix in thoroughly.

3 In a screw-top jar, shake together the sunflower oil, orange juice and spring onion (scallion). Pour the dressing over the watercress and carrot and serve.

Casseroled Potatoes

Supplies 0.2g fat and 150 calories per portion.

Imperial/metric	Serves 4	American
	a little oil for greasing	
1 small	onion	1 small
1½ lb (675g)	potatoes, scrubbed and thinly sliced	4 cups
8 fl oz (240ml)	skimmed milk	1 cup
1	bay leaf	1
	freshly ground black pepper	
3 tbs	fresh parsley, chopped	3 tbs

1 Peel the onion. Cut in half and slice thinly into semi-circles.
2 Preheat the oven to 375°F/190°C (Gas Mark 5).
3 Brush a shallow ovenproof dish with a little oil. Arrange the potato and onion slices neatly in

the dish, put the bay leaf in the centre and season liberally with freshly ground black pepper.
4 Pour the milk over and cover tightly with foil. Bake for 45–50 minutes until the potatoes are soft. Serve sprinkled with the chopped parsley.

Spinach and Mushroom Salad

Dark and nutritious spinach is good raw as well as lightly cooked.
Mushrooms make a good contrast in colour and texture.

Supplies 2.7g fat and 45 calories per portion.

Imperial/metric	Serves 4	American
½ lb (225g)	fresh spinach	5 cups
4 oz (100g)	mushrooms, thinly sliced	1½ cups
2 tsp	sunflower oil	2 tsp
½	lemon, juice of	½
	freshly ground black pepper	
½ tsp fresh	thyme	½ tsp fresh
or ¼ tsp dried		*or* ¼ tsp dried

1 Wash the spinach thoroughly and trim away any coarse stems or yellow leaves. Shred into ½-in (1-cm) wide strips.
2 Mix the mushrooms with the spinach.

3 In a screw-top jar, shake together the sunflower oil, lemon juice, freshly ground black pepper and thyme. Pour this dressing over the spinach and mushrooms and toss thoroughly.

Chapter 7

Home Baking

It's difficult to visualize treats without fat. By their very nature cakes and biscuits are high in fat and sugar — two undesirable ingredients in a healthy diet. Try to cut down on sweet foods like these, which serve little purpose other than supplying extra calories and satisfying our sweet tooth. For occasional treats, though, here are some recipes using wholemeal (whole wheat) flour, which supplies extra fibre, vitamins and minerals missing from refined white flour. They are also low in fat, made so by drastically cutting down the amount of margarine or butter added during mixing and keeping an eye on the amount of sugar used, too! Honey is a good alternative to sugar as it has a distinctive taste, adds a deep golden colour to baked goodies and is more concentrated in sweetness, so weight for weight, less is required for the same level of sweetness.

Cutting down on fat in cakes poses several problems. Fat contributes to the risen structure of a cake, to its soft texture and to its keeping qualities. These cakes depend on different ingredients for their lightness so will not keep fresh for longer than a day or two — but this is not usually a problem!

Biscuits lack crispness when made without fat. Lowest in fat and less sweet than most are digestives. The recipe in this chapter is simple and economical and the biscuits will keep fresh for several days if kept in an air-tight container.

Finally, there is a foolproof recipe for wholemeal (whole wheat) bread. Quicker than many recipes, it produces a light, well-risen loaf that is cheaper and tastier than bought bread.

Banana Cake

A light, moist cake. Eat within two days and keep wrapped in foil.

Supplies 0.4g fat and 100 calories per slice.

Imperial/metric	*Makes 10 slices*	American
3 tbs	clear honey	3 tbs
1	banana, mashed	1
4 oz (100g)	carrots, scrubbed and finely grated	⅔ cup
2 oz (50g)	dates, finely chopped	½ cup
6 oz (175g)	wholemeal/whole wheat flour	1½ cups
1½ tsp	baking powder	1½ tsp
¼ tsp	cinnamon	¼ tsp
¼ pt (150ml)	skimmed milk	⅔ cup
2	free-range egg whites	2

1 Preheat the oven to 325°F/170°C (Gas Mark 3).

2 Lightly grease a 2 lb (900g) loaf tin (pan) and dust with a little wholemeal (whole wheat) flour.

3 Put the honey in a large mixing bowl. Add the banana and beat together well. Stir in the carrots and dates. Sift in the flour, baking powder and cinnamon and then tip the bran remaining in the sieve into the bowl.

4 Add the milk and mix to a batter. Whisk the egg whites until stiff and fold them into the mixture. Pour it into the prepared tin (pan) and smooth the top.

5 Bake in the centre of the preheated oven for 35–40 minutes until golden brown and just firm to the touch. Cool it slightly in the tin, then turn it out (unmold it) and let it finish cooling on a wire cooling rack.

Fruity Fingers

A moist, slightly heavy texture but with a rich fruity flavour. Ideal for packed lunches.

Each one supplies 0.6g fat and 110 calories.

Imperial/metric	*Makes 10*	American
½ lb (225g)	cooking apples, peeled, cored and sliced	1½ cups
3 oz (75g)	wholemeal/whole wheat flour	¾ cup
½ tsp	baking powder	½ tsp
½ tsp	mixed spice	½ tsp
¼ tsp	ground cinnamon	¼ tsp
2 oz (50g)	rolled oats	½ cup
4 oz (100g)	sultanas/golden seedless raisins	⅔ cup
2 oz (50g)	raisins	⅓ cup
2 oz (50g)	currants	½ cup
¼ pt (150ml)	skimmed milk	⅔ cup
1	free-range egg white	1

1 Preheat the oven to 350°F/180°C (Gas Mark 4).

2 Lightly grease a shallow 8-in (20cm) square cake tin (pan) and dust with flour.

3 Put the cooking apple slices in a saucepan with a little water. Cook them gently over a low heat until they are soft and pulpy. Beat until smooth.

4 Sift the flour with the baking powder and spices into a mixing bowl, tipping the bran remaining in the sieve back into the bowl. Stir in the rolled oats, sultanas (golden seedless raisins), raisins and currants.

5 Pour in the apple purée and skimmed milk and beat together thoroughly. Whisk the egg white until stiff and fold it into the mixture. Pour it into the prepared tin (pan) and bake in the centre of the oven for 35–40 minutes until golden brown and firm to the touch. Leave it to cool in the tin on a wire rack before removing and cutting it into fingers.

Swiss Roll (Jelly Roll)

A nice light mixture that can be varied by adding either 1 teaspoon decaffeinated instant coffee mixed with 1 teaspoon water or substitute ½ oz (13g) flour with carob flour.

Supplies 11.5g fat and 65 calories for each piece.

Imperial/metric	*Makes 8 pieces*	American
2	free-range eggs	2
1	free-range egg white	1
3 tbs	clear honey	3 tbs
3 oz (75g)	wholemeal/whole wheat flour	¾ cup
3 tbs	no-added sugar jam/jelly	3 tbs

1 Preheat the oven to 425°F/220°C (Gas Mark 7).

2 Grease and line a swiss roll tin (jelly roll pan) with greaseproof (waxed) paper.

3 Put the eggs and egg white in a large bowl with the honey. Whisk together until the mixture is pale, thick and smooth (if using a hand whisk put the bowl over a pan of hot water to speed up the whisking process). The mixture is ready when the letter 'W' can be trailed in the mixture, with first stroke still visible when you make the last.

4 Sift in the flour and fold in gently but thoroughly with a metal spoon. Pour the mixture into the prepared tin (pan) and bake in the preheated oven for 8–10 minutes until the mixture springs back when touched and has shrunk away from the sides of the tin (pan).

5 Quickly turn the cake out of the tin (pan) onto a sheet of greaseproof (waxed) paper. Peel back the paper used to line the tin (pan) from the cake and spread the jam (jelly) over the cake. Trim off ¼-in (7mm) all round to neaten the edges of the cake. Make a small cut ½-in away from the edge nearest to you, and roll up from there using the greaseproof (waxed) paper to roll the sponge tightly. Leave to cool on a wire rack before serving.

Bara Brith

*Rather than relying on traditional cakes for treats, use recipes that have a
lower proportion of fat and are free or very low in egg content. This tea
bread doesn't need butter to taste good, if liked, spread with a little low-
sugar fruit jam.*

Supplies 2.5g fat and 125 calories per slice.

Imperial/metric	*Makes 10 slices*	American
½ lb (225g)	wholemeal/whole wheat flour	2 cups
1 oz (25g)	soft vegetable margarine, high in PUFA	2 tbs
1 tsp	mixed spice	1 tsp
¼ tsp	ground nutmeg	¼ tsp
2 oz (50g)	sultanas/golden seedless raisins	⅓ cup
3 oz (75g)	raisins	½ cup
1	lemon, grated rind of	1
6 fl oz (180ml)	skimmed milk	⅔ cup plus 2 tbs
½ oz (13g)	fresh yeast	1¼ tbs
1 tsp	clear honey	1 tsp
1 tsp and 1 tsp	clear honey and boiling water, to glaze	1 tsp and 1 tsp

1 Sift the flour into a mixing bowl and tip the bran remaining in the sieve back into the bowl. Rub (cut) in the margarine until the mixture resembles fine breadcrumbs.
2 Stir in the spices, fruits and grated lemon rind.
3 Heat the milk until it is just warm to the touch and stir in the yeast and honey. Let the yeast dissolve before pouring the mixture onto the dry ingredients.
4 Mix everything together to form a soft dough and then put it on a lightly floured surface and knead until the dough is soft and smooth. Put it in a bowl, covered, and leave to prove (rise) in a warm place (it should take about 1–1¼ hours).
5 Knead the dough lightly and gently pull it into an oblong three times as wide as a 1 lb (455g) loaf tin (pan). Fold the dough into three and drop it into the greased tin (pan). Cover it and leave in a warm place for 20–25 minutes until it has doubled in size. Heat the oven to 450°F/230°C (Gas Mark 8).
6 Glaze the top of the bara brith with a little skimmed milk and bake for 25 minutes. Test the loaf by turning it out of the tin. If it sounds hollow when it is tapped on the bottom, it is ready. Brush it with the honey and water glaze and leave it to cool on a wire cooling rack.

Digestive Biscuits (Cookies)

Many biscuits (cookies) are very high in fat. This simple recipe has a relatively small amount of fat and, rather than it being saturated as is the case with most commercial brands, uses a margarine high in polyunsaturated fatty acids.

Supplies 2.3g fat and 45 calories per biscuit.

Imperial/metric	Makes 20	American
3½ oz (88g)	wholemeal/whole wheat flour	scant cup
1½ oz (38g)	fine oatmeal	generous ¼ cup
½ tsp	baking powder	½ tsp
pinch	sea salt	pinch
2 oz (50g)	soft vegetable margarine, high in PUFA	¼ cup
1 tbs	Muscovado sugar	1 tbs
2–3 tbs	skimmed milk to mix	2–3 tbs

1 Preheat the oven to 350°F/180°C (Gas Mark 4) and lightly grease two baking trays (sheets).
2 Sift the flour, oatmeal, baking powder and salt into a mixing bowl and tip the bran remaining in the sieve back into the bowl. Rub (cut) the margarine into the mixture until it resembles fine breadcrumbs.
3 Stir in the sugar and mix in the milk with the blade of a knife. Bring it together with the fingers and knead it lightly.
4 Roll out the dough on a lightly floured surface to ⅛-in (3-mm) thickness. Stamp out rounds using a 3-in (7.5-cm) cutter.
5 Put the biscuits (cookies) on baking trays (sheets) and prick with a fork. Bake in the centre of the oven for 15 minutes until they are just turning brown at the edges. Transfer them to wire cooling racks to cool.

Oat Cakes

Save money and get the benefit of oat fibre by making your own oat cakes.
They are delicious as savoury crackers.

Supplies 3g fat and 70 calories per oat cake.

Imperial/metric	*Makes 20*	American
8 oz (225g)	medium oatmeal	2 cups
2 oz (50g)	wholemeal/whole wheat flour	½ cup
1 tsp	baking powder	1 tsp
2 oz (50g)	soft vegetable margarine, high in PUFA	¼ cup
	boiling water to mix	

1 Preheat the oven to 375°F/190°C (Gas Mark 5).
2 Mix together the oatmeal, flour and baking powder.
3 Melt the margarine in a saucepan and stir it into the dry ingredients, adding enough boiling water to form a soft dough.
4 Put on a lightly floured surface and knead it until the dough is firm enough to roll out. Roll it out into a rectangle shape and either stamp out plain rounds with a cutter or neaten the edges of the rectangle and cut out triangular shapes.
5 Using a palette knife (narrow metal spatula) slip the oat cakes onto non-stick or lightly oiled baking trays (sheets) and sprinkle with a little extra oatmeal before baking for 10–15 minutes until they just turn a very light colour. Cool them on wire cooling racks.

Wholemeal (Whole Wheat) Bread

This basic recipe for wholemeal (whole wheat) bread is time-saving because it uses vitamin C to cut down on the time required to prove the dough (make it rise). The result is a light loaf. The dough can be used to bake individual rolls or as a base for pizzas.

This quantity of bread dough contains 2330 calories and around 34g fat. A bread roll will therefore supply 116 calories and 1.7g fat.

Imperial/metric	Makes 2 loaves or 20 rolls	American
1½ lb (675g)	wholemeal/whole wheat flour	6 cups
1 tsp	sea salt	1 tsp
1 oz (25g)	soft vegetable margarine, high in PUFA	2 tbs
1 oz (25g)	fresh yeast	2½ tbs
15 fl oz (450ml)	lukewarm water	2 cups
25mg	vitamin C tablet, crushed	25mg
	Skimmed milk to glaze	

1 Mix the flour with the salt and rub (cut) in the margarine.

2 Crumble the yeast into the water and stir in the crushed vitamin C tablet. Mix well and pour the mixture on to the flour.

3 Draw together the flour and liquid with the fingers until it forms a dough.

4 Put the dough on to a lightly floured surface and knead for 10 minutes, adding more flour if required, to give a smooth and soft dough. Cover and leave to rest (let stand) for 10 minutes.

5 Meanwhile, lightly grease two 1-lb (455-g) loaf tins (pans). Preheat the oven to 450°F/ 230°C (Gas Mark 8).

6 Cut the dough in half. Shape one half into an oblong, three times the width of the tin (pan). Fold the left and right thirds over the centre and, with the seam underneath, put the dough in a tin (pan). Repeat with the remaining dough. Cover and leave to prove (rise) in a warm place until they have doubled in size (this takes around 25–35 minutes). The dough should spring back when touched with the fingertip.

7 Brush the top of each loaf with skimmed milk and bake at the top of the oven for 25–30 minutes. Test whether they are done by tipping each loaf out of the tin and tapping the underneath. If they sound hollow, then they are ready. Remove them from the tins (pans) and leave to cool on wire cooling racks.

8 To make bread rolls, divide the dough into 20 even-sized pieces. Shape each into a roll, place them spaced apart on greased baking trays (sheets) and cover. Leave them to prove (rise) in a warm place for 20–25 minutes then glaze and bake for 15–20 minutes.

Chapter 8

Entertaining Ideas

Most cooks take great pleasure in offering friends and relatives the best dishes in their culinary repertoire. Usually this means reaching for the cream and butter to concoct those extra-rich dishes reserved for special occasions, but if you are trying to limit the fat content of your diet there is no reason why you should suddenly undo all the good work when entertaining. There are many delicious dishes that can be made with small amounts of added fat which are good enough to grace any dining table.

The golden rule, as always, is to start with basic ingredients that are low in fat and to avoid adding extra fat when cooking and serving. That doesn't mean food has to be plain and simple; on the contrary there are many ways of transforming low-fat foods into impressive dishes. Take extra

trouble in presenting each dish attractively to delight the eye as well as the palate.

When eating out it is less easy to avoid eating too much — it is difficult to know just how dishes have been cooked. The safest bet is to choose plainly cooked food — grilled (broiled) rather than fried food, simple vegetables rather than elaborate, and fresh fruit, sorbets and fruit salads, all of which will be healthier alternatives to those cream-laden desserts on the groaning sweet trolley!

In this chapter there are 10 menus to help you keep down the fat content of food when catering for others. Some are formal, others less so. As always remember to balance each course so that the complete meal offers contrasting colours, flavours and textures.

Mushrooms Casseroled in Red Wine

Supplies 1.4g fat and 80 calories per portion.

Imperial/metric	Serves 4	American
1 tsp	olive oil	1 tsp
3 oz (75g)	onion, finely chopped	½ cup
2	cloves garlic, crushed/minced	2
½ lb (225g)	button mushrooms, finely chopped	3 cups
2 glasses	red wine	2 glasses
½	red pepper/sweet red pepper, deseeded and finely chopped	½
1	bay leaf	1
¼ tsp	dried thyme	¼ tsp
	freshly ground black pepper	

1 Put the olive oil in a saucepan and stir in the onion and garlic. Cook gently for 2 minutes. Now add the chopped mushrooms and cook for a further minute.

2 Pour in the red wine, add the red pepper (sweet red pepper), bay leaf and thyme. Cover and simmer for 40 minutes. Season to taste with freshly ground black pepper and serve with wholemeal (whole wheat) bread.

Tropical Chicken

A hint of curry spices and a touch of sweetness give this chicken dish a special flavour.

Supplies 9g fat and 240 calories per portion.

Imperial/metric	Serves 4	American
½ lb (225g)	carrots	½ lb
1 tsp	sunflower oil	1 tsp
2	frozen cubes vegetable stock	2
1 large	onion, finely chopped	1 large
2	celery sticks/stalks, finely chopped	2
2	cloves garlic, crushed/minced	2
½ tsp	ground coriander	½ tsp
½ tsp	ground cumin	½ tsp
1 lb (450g)	chicken, boned, skinned and cut into bite-sized pieces	1 lb
1 pt (600ml)	vegetable or chicken stock	2½ cup
8 fl oz (240ml)	pineapple juice	1 cup
3 tbs	tomato purée/paste	3 tbs
3 oz (75g)	dried apricots, chopped	½ cup
4 tbs	sweetcorn kernels	4 tbs
2	bay leaves	2
1	green pepper/sweet green pepper deseeded and chopped	1
2 tsp	cornflour/cornstarch, to thicken	2 tsp
1	banana, sliced	1
	freshly ground black pepper	

1 Scrub the carrots and cut them into fine matchsticks, 1 in (2.5cm) long.

2 Heat the oil and frozen cubes of stock, then lower the heat and add the onion, celery and garlic. Cook them gently for 3 minutes without browning. Stir in the coriander and cumin and cook for 1 minute.

3 Add the chicken and toss in the mixture so that it takes up some of the colour. Add the stock, pineapple juice, tomato purée (paste), apricots, sweetcorn and bay leaves. Bring to the boil, cover, reduce the heat and simmer for 1 hour.

4 Add the green pepper (sweet green pepper) to the pan. If the liquid needs thickening, mix the cornflour (cornstarch) with cold water and stir into the pan; let it boil then lower the heat, stir in the banana slices and season to taste with freshly ground black pepper. Serve at once with boiled rice.

Raspberry Whip

A tangy, super-smooth dessert.

Supplies 0.2g fat and 55 calories per portion.

Imperial/metric	Serves 4	American
¾ lb (325g)	raspberries, washed	2½ cups
8 fl oz (240ml)	natural/unsweetened yogurt	1 cup
2 tsp	clear honey	2 tsp
2	free-range egg whites	2

1 Put the raspberries into the goblet of a liquidizer (blender) with the yogurt and honey and blend until smooth.
2 Pour into a bowl. Whisk the egg whites until stiff and, using a metal spoon, fold them into the raspberry mixture. Pour the whip into serving glasses and chill overnight.

Avocado and Orange Salad

Arranged on individual plates this looks attractive and appetizing but remember that avocados have a very high natural fat content — use sparingly.

Supplies 1.4g fat and 170 calories per portion.

Imperial/metric	Serves 4	American
2	avocados	2
2	oranges	2
4 oz (100g)	low-fat soft cheese	½ cup
1-in (2.5-cm) piece	cucumber, grated	1-in piece
	freshly ground black pepper	
1 tbs *or* ½ tsp	chives, chopped, *or* dill seeds	1 tbs *or* 1 tsp

1 Halve the avocados and remove the stone (pit) from each. Peel and cut the flesh into slices.
2 Peel the oranges and remove any pith. Arrange the segments in a ring with the avocado slices on four small plates, leaving space in the centre for the dressing.

3 Put the cheese in a bowl and mix the cucumber with it. Season to taste with freshly ground black pepper and add the chives or dill seeds. Divide the dressing between the four plates, spooning it into the centre of the avocado and orange rings. Serve at once.

Rich Vegetable Casserole

Supplies under 1g fat and 140 calories per portion.

Imperial/metric	Serves 4	American
4 oz (100g)	onion, finely chopped	⅔ cup
2	celery sticks/stalks, chopped	2
6 oz (175g)	carrots, scrubbed and sliced	1 cup
½ pt (300ml)	vegetable stock	1⅓ cup
1 small	cauliflower, divided into florets	1 small
1 small	aubergine/eggplant, sliced	1 small
½ lb (225g)	canned red kidney beans, drained	1⅓ cup
½ pt (300ml)	tomato juice	1⅓ cup
½ pt (300ml)	red wine	1⅓ cup
2	bay leaves	2
sprig fresh *or* ½ tsp	thyme	sprig fresh *or* ½ tsp
4 oz (100g)	green cabbage, shredded	1 cup
2 tsp	cornflour/cornstarch, to thicken	2 tsp
	freshly ground black pepper	

1 Sauté the onion, celery and carrots in 3 tbs of the vegetable stock in a large saucepan, cooking them gently for 3 minutes.

2 Add the aubergine (eggplant) and cauliflower florets to the pan with the remaining stock, red kidney beans, tomato juice, red wine and herbs. Bring to the boil then simmer gently for 15 minutes.

3 Stir in the cabbage and cook for a further 4 minutes. Thicken the mixture with the cornflour (cornstarch) mixed with a little cold water. Season generously with freshly ground black pepper and serve at once with baked potatoes or rice.

Fruit Sorbet

Sorbets are light, refreshing and low in calories. Rather than using refined white sugar, this recipe is based on fruit sugar (fructose). Fructose is nature's sweetest sugar and so less needs to be used in a recipe to give the same amount of sweetness. Most sugars in this book are of the raw cane variety, but imagine how a delicate sorbet would be marred by brown sugar! Fructose is available from health food stores and some chemists (drug stores).

Purées of almost any fruit can be converted into sorbets. Try serving more tangy fruit sorbets as a second course in an impressive four-course meal. Grapefruit, orange and lemon are ideal for this. Serve a scoop of two contrasting sorbets together — pale pink raspberry, for example, with cool green melon.

Imperial/metric	Serves 4	American
2 oz (50g)	fructose	½ cup
¼ pt (150ml)	cold water	⅔ cup
1 lb (450g)	soft fruit of your choice	1 lb
2	free-range egg whites	2

1 Put the fructose and water in a small pan and heat gently until the fructose has dissolved. Boil for one minute then remove from the heat and leave to cool.
2 Prepare your chosen fruit. Peel, chop and purée (cooking it if required). Sieve (strain) to remove any pips (tiny seeds) or unwanted skins.
3 Put the fructose syrup and fruit purée in a blender goblet and blend until smooth.

4 Pour it into a shallow plastic container and freeze for 3–4 hours until the mixture is just mushy.
5 Beat it with a fork to break up any ice crystals. Whisk the egg whites until stiff and fold them into the fruit mixture with a metal spoon. Return to the freezer and freeze until firm (about 3 hours). Spoon or scoop into individual serving glasses.

MENU 3

Italian Tomato and Courgette (Zucchini) Soup
with wholemeal (whole wheat) bread
Baked Trout, with potatoes and green vegetables
Melon and Grape Dessert

Italian Tomato and Courgette (Zucchini) Soup

Use a small amount of good-quality olive oil to give this light soup a rich flavour.

Supplies 1.2g fat and 40 calories per portion.

Imperial/metric	*Serves 4*	American
3 oz (75g)	onion, finely chopped	½ cup
2	cloves garlic, crushed/minced	2
1 tsp	olive oil	1 tsp
2	frozen cubes vegetable stock	2
¾ tsp dried	marjoram *or* basil, chopped if fresh	¾ tsp dried
or 1½ tsp fresh		*or* 1½ tsp fresh
1	bay leaf	1
1 lb (450g) fresh	tomatoes, skinned and chopped	1 lb fresh
or 14-oz (397-g) tin		*or* 14-oz can
12 fl oz (360ml)	vegetable stock	1½ cups
6 oz (175g)	courgettes/zucchini	generous 2 cups
4 tbs	fresh parsley, chopped	4 tbs
	freshly ground black pepper	

1 Sauté the onion and garlic together in the olive oil and frozen stock cubes for 1 minute.
2 Add the marjoram or basil, tomatoes and stock and bring to the boil. Reduce the heat and simmer for 20 minutes.

3 Wipe the courgettes (zucchini) and cut into matchsticks, each 1 in (2.5cm) long. Add to the soup and cook for a further 5 minutes. Add the parsley and season to taste with the freshly ground black pepper. Serve at once.

Baked Trout

Trout contains less fat than oily fish and slightly more than white fish like cod and plaice (flounder). Its rich flavour is offset by lemon juice in this simple and speedy recipe. Keep the heads on for cooking as the eyes help to indicate when the fish is cooked — when they turn opaque the fish is ready.

Supplies 10g of fat and 320 calories per portion.

Imperial/metric	Serves 4	American
4 × ½ lb (225g)	trout	4 × ½ lb
1	lemon, juice of	1
2 tbs	wholemeal/whole wheat flour	2 tbs
	freshly ground black pepper	

1 Ask the fishmonger (fish merchant) to clean the trout. Wash each well, removing any blood that remains inside. Pat dry with kitchen paper (paper towels). Preheat the oven to 450°F/ 230°C (Gas Mark 8), letting it heat up fully.

2 Brush the insides of each trout with the lemon juice and lightly brush the outside skin, too. Put the flour on a plate and season with the pepper. Toss each trout in the flour.

3 Lay a sheet of foil on a baking tray (sheet) and arrange the trout on top. When the oven has heated up, put the tray (sheet) on the top shelf and bake for 7 minutes. Turn the trout and return to the oven for a further 2 minutes, basting with the juices that run from the fish. Serve at once with baked potatoes and a green vegetable or side salad.

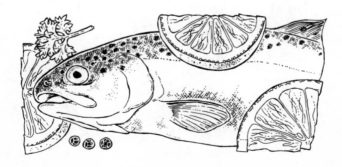

Melon and Grape Dessert

Choose the delicately coloured Galia melon for this pretty dessert.

Supplies a trace of fat and 90 calories per portion.

Imperial/metric	Serves 4	American
1 small	Galia melon	1 small
4	nectarines	4
4	apricots	4
6 oz (175g)	small seedless white grapes	generou cup
2 *or* ¼ pt	oranges, juice of *or* orange juice	2 *or*
(150ml) fresh		⅔ cup fresh
1 tbs	Cointreau, optional	1 tbs
	natural/unsweetened yogurt to serve	

1 Cut the melon into quarters and remove the seeds. Either remove the flesh using a melon scoop or peel and cut into bite-sized pieces.
2 Halve the nectarines, remove the stones (pits) and dice the flesh. Repeat with the apricots.

3 Mix all the fruit together in a bowl and add the grapes, orange juice and Cointreau, if using. Cover and chill for 30 minutes to let the flavours mingle. Serve with the natural (unsweetened) yogurt.

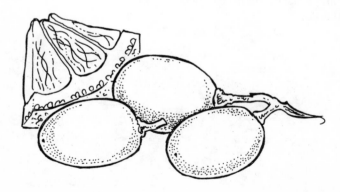

MENU 4

Grilled (Broiled) Grapefruit
Courgette (Zucchini) and Nut Loaf with
potatoes and a side salad
Jellied Fruit Cups with yogurt

Grilled (Broiled) Grapefruit

Supplies a trace of fat and 105 calories per portion.

Imperial/metric	*Serves 4*	American
2	grapefruit	2
4 tbs	dry sherry	4 tbs
4 tbs	demerara/raw brown sugar	4 tbs

1 Cut the grapefruit in half and cut between the segments using a small sharp knife. Cut round the outside, slipping the knife under the central core. Remove any pips (seeds).
2 Sprinkle a tbs of the dry sherry and a tbs of the sugar on top of each half.
3 Heat the grill (broiler) to very hot. Put the prepared grapefruit on the grill (broiler) pan and grill (broil) until the sugar caramelizes lightly and serve at once.

Courgette (Zucchini) and Nut Loaf

Supplies 11g fat and 230 calories per portion.

Imperial/metric	Serves 4	American
4 oz (100g)	onion, finely chopped	⅔ cup
1 tsp	oil	1 tsp
3	celery sticks/stalks, finely chopped	3
6 oz (175g)	carrots, scrubbed and grated	1 cup
6 oz (175g)	courgettes/zucchini, grated	generous 2 cups
6 oz (175g)	fresh wholemeal/whole wheat breadcrumbs	3 cups
2 oz (50g)	peanuts, ground	½ cup
2½ oz (63g)	hazelnuts, ground	generous ½ cup
½ tsp	fresh rosemary, chopped	½ tsp
½ tsp	dried thyme	½ tsp
	freshly ground black pepper	
1	free-range egg	1
2 tbs	vegetable stock	2 tbs
1 tbs	tomato purée/paste	1 tbs

1 Lightly grease a 2 lb (900g) loaf tin (pan).

2 Preheat the oven to 375°F/190°C (Gas Mark 5).

3 Cook the onion over a low heat in the oil for 2 minutes, then put it into a large mixing bowl.

4 Add the celery, carrot and courgette (zucchini) to the bowl.

5 Stir in the breadcrumbs, peanuts and hazelnuts, rosemary and thyme and mix together thoroughly. Season with freshly ground black pepper and bind the mixture with the egg, stock and tomato purée (paste). Put it into the tin (pan) and smooth the top. Cover with foil and bake at the top of the preheated oven for 30 minutes. Remove the foil and continue cooking for a further 10 minutes without the foil.

6 Turn the loaf out (unmold it) and serve sliced, either hot or cold. The mixture could also be baked in a ring mould (tube pan) and served with a salad in the centre.

Jellied Fruit Cups

Choose good-quality fruits for this simple dessert and arrange them attractively.

Supplies only a trace of fat and 55 calories per portion.

Imperial/metric	Serves 4	American
small bunch	black grapes	small bunch
1 small	honeydew melon	1 small
1	peach *or* orange	1
1 pt (600ml)	white grape *or* apple juice	2½ cups
½ oz (13g)	gelatine *or* equivalent vegetarian setting agent	1 packet
	natural/unsweetened yogurt to serve	

1 Wash the fruit well. Halve and deseed the grapes. Cut the melon in half, scoop out the seeds and remove the flesh with a melon baller. Cut the peach or orange flesh into small dice. Arrange attractively in four individual glass serving dishes.

2 Heat the fruit juice and dissolve the gelatine or other setting agent in it. Pour this over the fruit — gently so as not to disturb the pattern. Chill until set, preferably overnight, and serve with natural (unsweetened) yogurt.

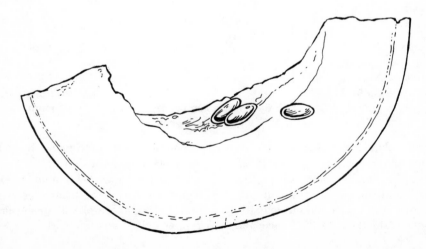

MENU 5
Beans à la Grecque
Mushroom-stuffed Plaice (Flounder) with
potatoes and a green vegetable
Fresh Fruit Salad with yogurt

Beans à la Grecque

*Mushrooms, courgettes (zucchini) and cauliflower florets can also be served
in this way to make a chilled starter.*

Supplies only a trace of fat and 25 calories per portion.

Imperial/metric	*Serves 4*	American
2	cloves garlic, crushed/minced	2
2	tomatoes, fresh, ripe and skinned	2
1 tbs	tomato purée/paste	1 tbs
2 tbs	dry white wine or dry/hard cider	2 tbs
4 fl oz (120ml)	water	½ cup
4	coriander seeds	4
1	bay leaf	1
¼ tsp dried	thyme	¼ tsp dried
or ½ tsp fresh		*or* ½ tsp fresh
¼ tsp dried	oregano	¼ tsp dried
or ½ tsp fresh		*or* ½ tsp fresh
¾ lb (325g)	French/fine green beans	¾ cup
	freshly ground black pepper	

1 Put the garlic and the tomatoes in a saucepan with the tomato purée (paste), wine or cider, coriander seeds, bay leaf, thyme and oregano, bring to the boil and simmer for 5 minutes.
2 Meanwhile, trim the beans and cut into 1-in (2.5-cm) lengths. Add them to the sauce and simmer until just soft. Remove the beans and rub the sauce through a sieve.
3 Heat the sauce for 5 minutes to reduce it, then pour it over the beans and leave to cool. Chill overnight. Season with freshly ground black pepper before serving.

Mushroom-stuffed Plaice (Flounder)

Choose small plaice (flounder) for this dish, as they are left whole.

Supplies 2.7g fat and 130 calories per portion.

Imperial/metric	Serves 4	American
4 small	plaice/flounder, whole	4 small
3 oz (75g)	onion, finely chopped	½ cup
1 tsp	sunflower oil	1 tsp
3 oz (75g)	button mushrooms	1½ cup
½ tsp dried	thyme	½ tsp dried
or 1 tsp fresh		*or* 1 tsp fresh
1 tbs	fresh parsley, chopped	1 tbs
3 oz (75g)	fresh wholemeal/whole wheat breadcrumbs	1½ cups
1 tbs	vegetable stock	1 tbs
	freshly ground black pepper	

1 Ask the fishmonger (fish merchant) to clean the plaice (flounder). Wash them and pat dry with kitchen paper (paper towels). Put the fish dark side down on a chopping board and, with a sharp knife, make a cut along the backbone. Gently ease away the flesh either side so you are left with two pockets to stuff.

2 Preheat the oven to 375°F/190°C (Gas Mark 5).

3 To make the stuffing, sauté the onion in the oil gently for 2 minutes. Add the mushrooms and continue to cook until the juices run.

4 Put the onion and mushroom mixture in a bowl, add the remaining ingredients and mix in thoroughly.

5 Stuff the pockets you have made in each fish firmly, then arrange them in a shallow, ovenproof dish with a tbs of cold water in the bottom. Cover with foil and bake in the centre of the preheated oven for 20 minutes. Serve straight away.

Fresh Fruit Salad

This dessert can be served at any time of the year and is equally suitable for simple family meals and more formal dinner parties. Simply vary the fruit used and, for a more exotic dish, add some chopped mango, kiwi fruit or papaya. Serve with yogurt rather than cream to keep down the fat content.

Supplies only a trace of fat and around 90 calories each.

Imperial/metric	Serves 4	American
small bunch	grapes, white or black	small bunch
2	oranges	2
2	peaches, nectarines or pears	2
½	melon	½
a few	strawberries *or* raspberries, if in season	a few
3	red-skinned eating/dessert apples	3
1	lemon, juice of	1
3 tbs	orange juice	3 tbs
1	banana	1

1 Wash the grapes, halve and remove the pips (tiny seeds). Peel the oranges, removing the pith, and cut into chunks. Halve and chop the peaches or nectarines (if using pears, prepare with the apples and place in a little lemon juice). Scoop out the melon seeds and dice the flesh. Mix all the fruit in a bowl as you prepare it.

2 Core and chop the apples finely, mixing them with the lemon juice to stop them browning. Add them to the bowl. Pour the orange juice over and stir it in well. Chill before serving and, when ready to serve, slice the banana into the bowl.

Mango with Prawns

Supplies 0.9g fat and 120 calories per portion.

Imperial/metric	Serves 4	American
2 small	mangoes	2 small
2 oz (50g)	low-fat soft cheese	¼ cup
3 tbs	low-fat natural/unsweetened yogurt	3 tbs
½ tsp	ground cumin seeds	½ tsp
¼ tsp	ground coriander	¼ tsp
pinch	cayenne pepper	pinch
	freshly ground black pepper	
6 oz (175g)	prawns, shelled/shucked	6 oz

1 Cut the mangoes in half and remove the stones (pits). Wipe the outsides.
2 Mix together the soft cheese, yogurt, cumin, coriander and cayenne pepper and season with freshly ground black pepper. Stir in the prawns.
3 Fill the centres of each mango half with the prawn mixture and chill until required.

Chicken Provençal

Choose skinned and boned chicken breasts for this simple dish. The addition of dry (hard) cider or wine adds extra richness to the sauce, but for a more economical dish, use extra stock as a substitute.

Supplies 5.8g of fat and 260 calories per portion.

Imperial/metric	Serves 4	American
4	chicken breasts, boned	4
4 oz (100g)	onion, finely chopped	⅔ cup
1	clove garlic, crushed/minced	1
1	celery stick/stalk, chopped	1
1	green pepper/sweet green pepper, deseeded and chopped	1
4 oz (100g)	button mushrooms, sliced	1½ cups
2×14-oz (397-g) tin *or* 2lb fresh	tomatoes, skinned if fresh	2×14-oz can *or* 2 lb fresh
¼ pt (150ml)	vegetable stock	⅔ cup
¼ pt (150ml)	dry/hard cider *or* dry white wine	⅔ cup
1 tsp dried *or* 2 tsp fresh	oregano *or* marjoram	1 tsp dried *or* 2 tsp fresh
6 oz (175g)	courgettes/zucchini, sliced	4 cups
	freshly ground black pepper	
2 tbs	fresh parsley, chopped	2 tbs

1 Preheat the oven to 375°F/190°C (Gas Mark 5).
2 Wash the chicken breasts and remove the skin.
3 Put the onion, garlic, celery, pepper (sweet pepper) and mushrooms into a casserole dish with the chicken. Add the tomatoes, stock, cider or wine and the oregano or marjoram. Mix together well, cover tightly and bake in the preheated oven for 1 hour.
4 Add the courgettes (zucchini) to the casserole. Cook for 20 more minutes, adding a little extra vegetable stock if necessary. Season to taste with freshly ground black pepper and sprinkle the parsley on top. Serve at once.

Apricot Fluff

*Dried apricots are nutritious and produce a tasty and tangy dessert when
mixed with low-fat soft cheese. Try using tofu, a soya-based product
available from health food stores, for a change.*

Supplies 2.5g fat and 170 calories each.

Imperial/metric	Serves 4	American
½ lb (225g)	dried apricots, soaked overnight in ½ pt (300ml/1⅓ cups) water	1⅔ cups
1	lemon, grated rind of	1
½-in (1-cm) piece	cinnamon stick	½-in piece
1 tbs	clear honey	1 tbs
6 oz (175g)	low-fat soft cheese *or* tofu	¾ cup
2	free-range egg whites	2
	twists of lemon, to garnish	

1 Put the soaked apricots (with their water), the lemon rind and cinnamon stick in a pan and cook gently for 15 minutes until soft. Remove the cinnamon and purée the fruit.
2 Stir the honey and low-fat soft cheese or tofu into the apricot purée and blend in well.

3 Whisk the egg whites until stiff, then fold them into the apricot mixture. Pour the fluff into four serving glasses and decorate each one with a lemon twist. Chill for 30 minutes before serving.

MENU 7

Spring Cocktail
Hot Chilli Beans with rice
Raisin-stuffed Apples with yogurt

Spring Cocktail

Supplies a trace of fat and 20 calories per portion.

Imperial/metric	Serves 4	American
½	honeydew melon	½
2	tomatoes, ripe	2
3-in (7.5-cm)	cucumber	3-in piece
1	lime, juice of	1
1 small	orange, juice of	1 small
1 tbs	mint, fresh	1 tbs

1 Cut away the flesh from the melon, discarding the seeds. Dice the flesh and put it in a bowl.
2 Cut the tomatoes into small cubes and dice the cucumber. Add them to the melon and pour the lime and orange juices over them.
3 Chop the mint finely and add it to the bowl. Cover and leave to marinate for at least an hour before serving in individual serving dishes.

Hot Chilli Beans

A vegetarian alternative to a favourite supper dish.

Supplies 1.5g fat and 210 calories per portion.

Imperial/metric	Serves 4	American
6 oz (175g)	onion, finely chopped	1 cup
6 oz (175g)	carrot, finely chopped	1 cup
1	celery stick/stalk, chopped	1
3	green chillies/green chili peppers, deseeded and very finely chopped	3
1	green pepper/sweet green pepper, deseeded and chopped	1
1	red pepper/sweet red pepper, deseeded and chopped	1
6 oz (175g)	red kidney beans, soaked overnight	¾ cup
3 oz (175g)	black kidney beans, soaked overnight	generous ¼ cup
2 lb (900g) fresh *or* 2×14-oz (397-g) tins	tomatoes, skinned if fresh	2 lb fresh *or* 2×14-oz cans
¼ pt (150ml)	vegetable stock	⅔ cup
¾ tsp	ground cumin seeds	¾ tsp
	freshly ground black pepper	

1 Put the onion, carrot, celery, chillies (chili peppers) and peppers (sweet peppers), in a large saucepan and add the drained red and black kidney beans, tomatoes, stock and cumin seeds. Cover the pan and bring to the boil. Boil for 10 minutes, then lower the heat.
2 Simmer steadily for 1¾–2 hours until the beans are just tender. Check from time to time during cooking to ensure that the mixture does not become too dry and, if necessary, add extra stock. Season to taste with freshly ground black pepper and serve hot with plain boiled long grain brown rice or baked potatoes and a crisp side salad.

Raisin-stuffed Apples

An old family favourite. Served topped with natural yogurt.

Supplies a trace of fat and 160 calories per portion.

Imperial/metric	Serves 4	American
4 even-sized	cooking apples	4 even-sized
4 oz (100g)	raisins	⅔ cup
2 tbs	clear honey	2 tbs

1 Preheat the oven to 400°F/200°C (Gas Mark 6).

2 Wash and core the apples. Slit the skins around the middle of the apples.

3 Put the apples in a shallow, ovenproof dish and put 3 tbs cold water in the bottom to stop them from sticking and becoming dry.

4 Spoon the raisins into the apple cavities and pour honey over each. Bake in the oven for 20–30 minutes until the apples are just soft. Watch the apples carefully as cooking times vary with the type of apple used. Test by inserting the blade of a small knife into the slit skin. If the apple is soft, it is ready to eat.

MENU 8
Savoury Peach
Salmon Parcels with new potatoes and vegetables
Poached Pears with yogurt

Savoury Stuffed Peach

This recipe is based on an idea sampled at a favourite hotel in Hope Cove, Devon.

Supplies 1g fat and 60 calories per portion.

Imperial/metric	Serves 4	American
4	ripe peaches	4
3 oz (75g)	low-fat soft cheese	scant ½ cup
1 tbs	fresh chives, chopped	1tbs
generous pinch	thyme	generous pinch
or 1 tsp fresh		*or* 1 tsp fresh
	freshly ground black pepper	
	sesame seeds	

1 Preheat the oven to 400°F/200°C (Gas Mark 6).
2 Halve the peaches and remove the stones (pits). In a bowl, mix together the low-fat soft cheese, herbs and freshly ground black pepper.
3 Fill the centre of each peach half with a little of the cheese mixture.

4 Put the peaches in a shallow, heatproof dish with 2 tbs water in the bottom. Cover with foil and bake in the centre of the preheated oven for 10 minutes. Remove the foil, sprinkle sesame seeds on top and cook for a further 5 minutes. Serve hot.

Salmon Parcels

Salmon baked in foil cooks in its own juices to bring out the full flavour of the fish. The slivers of root ginger make an interesting addition to this dish.

Supplies 20g fat and 355 calories per portion.

Imperial/metric	Serves 4	American
4×6-oz (175-g)	salmon steaks	4×6-oz
2 tbs	sultanas/golden seedless raisins	2 tbs
4 fine slivers	root ginger	4 fine slivers
	freshly ground black pepper	
2 tbs	fresh parsley, chopped	2 tbs

1 Preheat the oven to 400°F/200°C (Gas Mark 6).

2 Put each salmon steak in the centre of an 8-in (20-cm) square piece of foil. Sprinkle the sultanas in equal amounts over each portion. Put a sliver of ginger on top of each fish. Grind black pepper over each fish and firmly seal each parcel.

3 Put the parcels on a baking tray (sheet) and bake in the preheated oven for 20 minutes. Serve each parcel on a plate and open the foil a little at the top. Sprinkle the parsley inside each one.

Poached Pears

Supplies only a trace of fat and 44 calories per portion.

Imperial/metric	Serves 4	American
1 lb (450g)	pears (firm cooking pears)	1 lb
4	cloves	4
½-in (1-cm) piece	cinnamon stick	½-in piece
1	lemon, rind of, thinly sliced	1
	water to cover	
1 tbs	clear honey	1 tbs
	natural/unsweetened yogurt to serve	

1 Preheat the oven to 350°F/180°C (Gas Mark 4).
2 Wash the pears, halve them and remove the cores. Put them in a shallow ovenproof dish with the cloves, cinnamon and lemon rind and just cover with water. Dribble the honey over the top.
3 Cover and bake in the preheated oven for 1–1½ hours until tender. Serve hot with yogurt.

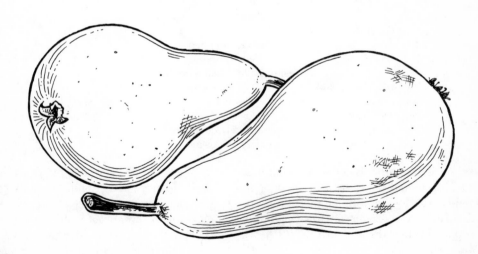

MENU 9: A Sunday Lunch

Pot Roast Chicken with casseroled potatoes
and two vegetables
Hazelnut and Banana Gâteau

Pot Roast Chicken

Cider is used to cook this chicken dish. Use either a casserole with a tight-fitting lid or cover tightly with foil so the bird cooks in the aromatic steam.

Supplies 6g fat and 330 calories per portion.

Imperial/metric	Serves 4	American
4 oz (100g)	long grain brown rice	½ cup
1	green pepper/sweet green pepper, deseeded and finely chopped	1
3 oz (75g)	raisins	½ cup
1 tbs	chives, chopped	1 tbs
1 tbs	dry/hard cider	1 tbs
	freshly ground black pepper	
3½–4-lb (1.6–1.8-k)	fresh free-range chicken	3½–4-lb
sprig fresh *or* ½ tsp dried	rosemary	sprig fresh *or* ½ tsp dried
2 oz (50g)	onion, finely chopped	⅓ cup
1	celery stick/stalk	1

1 Make the stuffing first. Boil the rice until it is just tender, drain and set aside. Add the pepper (sweet pepper) to the rice with the raisins, chives and 1 tbs of cider and season with freshly ground black pepper. Preheat the oven to 375°F/190°C (Gas Mark 5).

2 Wipe the chicken and pat dry with kitchen paper (paper towels). Stuff the body cavity with the rice mixture and put the chicken in a casserole or ovenproof dish.

3 Pour the rest of the cider over the chicken and divide the rosemary over the top. Season lightly with freshly ground black pepper. Add the onion and celery to the dish. Cover tightly, put in the centre of the oven and cook for 1¾–2 hours, basting every half hour with the stock. Remove the foil or lid 15 minutes from the end of cooking time so the chicken browns. Carve, removing the skin, and serve with the stock and a spoonful of stuffing.

Hazelnut and Banana Gâteau

It's hard to believe that this lighter than air gâteau contains no extra fat — its only drawback is the eggs it contains. Serve it on special occasions, and remember to use low-fat soft cheese or a set thick natural (unsweetened) yogurt for the filling.

Supplies 3.8g of fat and 120 calories per portion.

Imperial/metric	Serves 7	American
3	free-range eggs	3
3 oz (75g)	clear honey	4 tbs
2½ oz (63g)	wholemeal/whole wheat flour	generous ½ cup
½ oz (13g)	hazelnuts, ground	2½ tbs
4 oz (100g)	low-fat soft cheese	½ cup
½	lemon, juice of	½
2	bananas	2

1 Grease and line two 7-in (17.5-cm) sandwich cake tins (pans).

2 Preheat the oven to 425°F/220°C (Gas Mark 7).

3 Put the eggs and honey in a large mixing bowl and beat together (if beating by hand the mixture will thicken quicker if the bowl is placed over a pan of boiling water but this isn't necessary if using an electric mixer). Beat the mixture until it is thick, pale and smooth. Test by trailing the mixture into a letter W. If when you make the last stroke the first stroke is still visible, then the mixture is ready.

4 Sift the flour into the bowl with the egg and honey mixture tipping any bran left in the sieve back into the bowl. Add the ground hazelnuts. Fold the dry ingredients in gently using a metal spoon. When thoroughly mixed pour the mixture into the prepared tins (pans) and bake in the centre of the preheated oven for 15–20 minutes until just firm to the touch and when the cakes have shrunk away from the sides of the tins. Put them on wire cooking racks and leave to settle for a minute, then carefully turn them out (unmold) them and leave them to cool thoroughly.

5 When the cakes are quite cold, put the low-fat soft cheese in a bowl and add the lemon juice and the bananas. Mash them together and spread half this mixture on one half of the cake, sandwich the two together and spread the remainder on top. This cake will not keep and is best eaten really fresh so do not make it too far in advance of serving time.

MENU 10: An Informal Barbecue Party

Smoked Mackerel Dip with crudités
Spiced Fish Kebabs (Kabobs) *or*
Mixed Vegetable Kebabs (Kabobs)
with Spiced Mushroom Rice
Fruity Skewers

Smoked Mackerel Dip

*This easy-to-prepare dip makes a perfect starter for an informal supper if
served with crudités or strips of wholemeal (whole wheat) toast. If serving
with crudités, choose from celery, carrots, cauliflower florets, red or green
peppers (red or green sweet peppers), mushrooms, cucumber and fennel,
cutting all the vegetables into even pieces.*

Supplies 4.5g fat and 60 calories per portion.

Imperial/metric	*Serves 4–6*	American
6 oz (175g)	smoked mackerel fillets	6 oz
4 oz (100g)	low-fat soft cheese	½ cup
½	lemon, juice of	½
	freshly ground black pepper	
	fresh chives or parsley, chopped, to garnish	

1 Remove the flesh from the mackerel, peeling it away from the skin and taking out any bones, then roughly chop.
2 Mix the soft cheese with the mackerel and lemon juice and season to taste. Pound them together thoroughly until the mixture is smooth and well mixed. Chill until required, then garnish with the chives or parsley.

Spiced Fish Kebabs (Kabobs)

The best fish for kebabs (kabobs) is monkfish, but this tends to be expensive and may not always be available. As an alternative, chunky pieces of cod or haddock could be used. If liked, serve a mixed vegetable kebab (kabob) with these fish ones. Rice is the perfect accompaniment.

Supplies 2.3g fat and 170 calories each.

Imperial/metric	Serves 4	American
1¼ lb (550g)	monkfish *or* chunky cod *or* haddock fillet	1¼ lb
5 fl oz (150ml)	natural/unsweetened yogurt	⅔ cup
1 tsp	olive oil	1 tsp
½ tsp	ground coriander	½ tsp
½ tsp	ground cumin seeds	½ tsp
pinch	cayenne pepper	pinch
pinch	turmeric	pinch
	freshly ground black pepper	
2	onions, quartered	2

1 Wash the fish, cut it into pieces about 1 in (2.5cm) square and put it into a bowl.

2 Mix the yogurt, olive oil and spices and season to taste with freshly ground black pepper and pour it over the fish. Leave to marinate for 2–4 hours.

3 Arrange the onions and fish on skewers and have ready a barbecue or hot grill (broiler). Cook the kebabs (kabobs) for 10–15 minutes, basting them frequently with the marinade. Serve at once with the remaining marinade spooned over as a sauce.

Mixed Vegetable Kebabs (Kabobs)

Supplies 1.4g fat and 60 calories per portion.

Imperial/metric	Serves 4	American
1 medium	aubergine/eggplant	1 medium
	sea salt	
¾ lb (325g)	courgettes/zucchini	¾ lb
½ lb (225g)	button mushrooms	4 cups
1	green pepper/sweet green pepper	1
2 small	onions, quartered	2 small
4 medium	tomatoes, quartered	4 medium
	For the marinade:	
1	lemon, juice of	1
1	clove garlic, crushed/minced	1
1 tsp	olive oil	1 tsp
sprig fresh	rosemary, chopped if fresh	sprig fresh
or ¼ tsp dried		*or* ¼ tsp dried
	freshly ground black pepper	

1 First prepare the aubergine (eggplant). Cut it into slices ½ in (1cm) thick. Sprinkle with sea salt to draw out the bitterness and leave for 30 minutes. Wipe and pat dry and cut into chunks.
2 Mix together the marinade ingredients and put in a bowl with the aubergine (eggplant). Leave to marinade for 30 minutes.
3 Cut the courgettes (zucchini) into slices just under ½ in (1cm) thick. Wipe the mushrooms, deseed the pepper (sweet pepper) and cut it into ½ in (1cm) squares.
4 Have ready four skewers. Starting with a piece of courgette (zucchini) arrange all the vegetables on the skewers. Heat the grill (broiler) to very hot. Brush the kebabs (kabobs) with the marinade and cook for 15 minutes, turning and basting frequently. Alternatively, cook over a barbecue. Serve with rice and a salad.

Spiced Mushroom Rice

Supplies 0.7g fat and 200 calories per portion.

Imperial/metric	Serves 4	American
2	cloves garlic, crushed/minced	2
½-in (1-cm) cube	root ginger, peeled and grated	½-in cube
2 tbs	water	2 tbs
1 small	onion, chopped	1 small
½ tsp	ground cumin	½ tsp
pinch	cayenne pepper	pinch
½ lb (225g)	long grain brown rice	1 cup
18 fl oz (540ml)	vegetable stock	2⅓ cups
1	bay leaf	1
6 oz (175g)	mushrooms, chopped	2¼ cups
	freshly ground black pepper	

1 Put the garlic, ginger and water in a liquidizer (blender) and blend with the water until smooth.
2 Heat this paste in a saucepan and add the onion. Cook for 1 minute. Stir in the cumin and cayenne pepper and cook for a further minute. Add the rice and stir, coating the grains evenly.
3 Pour in the stock, add the bay leaf and mushrooms and bring to the boil. Reduce the heat and cook slowly for 25–30 minutes until all the liquid has been absorbed and the rice is just tender. Do not stir rice while cooking.
4 When tender, turn off the heat and leave the pan on the ring for a further 5 minutes. Season to taste with freshly ground black pepper and serve at once. This makes an ideal accompaniment to kebabs (kabobs) and all types of Indian dishes.

Fruity Skewers

A good way of finishing off a barbecue. Have ready a bowl of fruit pieces soaking in juice and ask guests to skewer their own selection and then cook them. Choose fairly firm-fleshed fruit that will not break up as it cooks.

Supplies only a trace of fat and 100 calories per portion.

Imperial/metric	*Serves 4*	American
1	melon	1
2	nectarines	2
1	lemon, juice of	1
1 small *or* small tin	pineapple pieces	1 small *or* small can
¼ pt (150ml)	fresh orange juice	⅔ cup
¼-in (0.5-cm) piece	cinnamon stick	¼-in piece
pinch	ground ginger	pinch

1 Cut the melon into quarters, scoop out the seeds and cut the flesh into large cubes. Halve the nectarines and cut into large cubes. Peel and slice the bananas. If fresh, peel and chop the pineapple; if tinned (canned), drain.
2 Mix together in a bowl and pour the orange juice over. Add the cinnamon and ginger and marinate for 30 minutes.
3 Skewer the pieces of fruit and cook over a barbecue for 5 minutes, turning them so they cook evenly.

Appendix 1:

The Fat and Calorie Contents of Food

All these figures are taken from McCance and Widdowson's *The Composition of Foods* by A. A. Paul and D. A. T. Southgate. The figures show the weight of fat (g) and the number of kilocalories in 100g (4 oz) of the food.

	Fat (g)	Calories
Dairy produce		
Full-fat milk	3.8	65
Skimmed milk	0.1	33
Single (light) cream	21.2	212
Double (heavy) cream	48.2	447
Whipping cream	35.0	332
Camembert cheese	23.2	300
Cheddar (New York, etc.) cheese	33.5	406
Danish Blue cheese	29.2	355
Edam	22.9	304
Stilton	40.0	462
Cottage cheese	4.0	96
Soft cheese	47.4	439
Yogurt	1.0	52
Eggs (approx. 2 size 4/2 medium)	10.9	147
yolk	30.5	339
white	Tr*	36

* Tr = Trace

	Fat (g)	Calories
Meat		
Bacon,		
grilled (broiled) gammon (ham) rasher, with fat	12.2	228
grilled (broiled) streaky rasher (fatty bacon), with fat	36.0	422
Beef		
grilled (broiled) rump steak, lean and fat	12.1	218
lean only	6.0	168
stewed mince (ground round)	16.2	221
roast sirloin (top round), lean and fat	21.2	284
lean only	9.1	192
stewed steak, lean and fat	11.0	223
Lamb,		
breast, roast lean and fat	37.1	410
lean only	16.6	252
cutlets, grilled (broiled) lean and fat (weighed with bone)	20.4	244
lean only	5.4	97
leg, roast lean and fat	17.9	266
lean only	8.1	191
shoulder, roast lean and fat	26.3	316
lean only	11.2	196
Pork,		
belly (side) rashers, grilled (broiled) lean and fat	34.8	398
loin chops, grilled (broiled) lean and fat (weighed with bone)	18.8	258
lean only	6.3	133
leg, roast lean and fat	19.8	286
Veal,		
fillet, roast	11.5	230
Poultry and game		
Chicken,		
boiled, meat only	7.3	183
roast, meat only	5.4	148
meat and skin	14.0	216
leg quarter (weighed with bone)	3.4	92

	Fat (g)	Calories
Duck,		
roast, meat only	9.7	189
meat, fat and skin	29.0	339
Pheasant, roast	9.3	213
Pigeon (squab), roast	13.2	230
Turkey,		
roast, meat only	2.7	140
roast, meat and skin	6.5	171
Rabbit, stewed	7.7	179

Offal

	Fat (g)	Calories
Lamb kidney, raw	2.7	90
Pig kidney, raw	2.7	90
Ox kidney, raw	2.6	86
Chicken liver, raw	6.3	135
Lamb liver, raw	10.3	179
Pig liver, raw	6.8	154

Meat products

	Fat (g)	Calories
Corned beef	12.1	217
Ham	5.1	120
Luncheon meat	26.9	313
Ham and pork, chopped	23.6	270
Liver sausage	26.9	310
Frankfurters	25.0	274
Salami	45.2	491
Beef sausages, fried	18.0	269
grilled (broiled)	17.3	265
Pork sausages, fried	24.5	317
grilled (broiled)	24.6	318
Beefburgers, fried	17.3	264
Cornish pasty	20.4	332
Pork pie	27.0	376
Sausage roll	36.2	479
Steak and kidney pie	21.2	323

	Fat (g)	Calories
Fish		
Cod,		
fried in batter	10.3	199
grilled (broiled)	1.3	95
poached	1.1	94
Haddock,		
fried	8.3	174
steamed	0.8	98
smoked, steamed	0.9	101
Halibut, steamed	4.0	131
Lemon sole (sole),		
fried	13.0	216
steamed	0.9	91
Plaice (flounder),		
fried in batter	18.0	279
steamed	1.9	93
Herring,		
fried (weighed with bones)	13.3	206
grilled (broiled) (weighed with bones)	8.8	135
Kipper, baked (weighed with bones)	6.2	111
Mackerel, fried (weighed with bones)	8.3	138
Salmon, steamed (weighed with bones and skin)	10.5	160
Sardines, canned in oil, fish only	13.6	217
Trout, brown, steamed (weighed with bones)	3.0	89
Tuna, canned in oil	22.0	289
Crab, boiled	5.2	127
Prawns (large shrimp), boiled	1.8	107
Scampi, fried	17.6	316
Shrimps (jumbo shrimp), boiled	2.4	117
Scallops (sea scallops), steamed	1.4	105
Cereals		
Barley	1.7	360
Wholemeal (whole wheat) flour	2.0	318
Oatmeal	8.7	401

	Fat (g)	Calories
Rice	1.0	361
Wholemeal (whole wheat) bread	2.7	216
Muesli	7.5	368
Shredded Wheat	3.0	324
Weetabix	3.4	340
Rye crispbread	2.1	321

Cakes, pastries and biscuits (cookies)

	Fat (g)	Calories
Digestives (Graham crackers)	20.5	471
Chocolate digestives (chocolate Graham crackers)	24.1	493
Fruit cake	12.9	354
Doughnuts	15.8	349
Scones	14.6	371
Fruit pie	15.5	369

Pulses (legumes)

	Fat (g)	Calories
Butter (lima) beans,		
raw	1.1	273
boiled	0.3	95
Haricot (navy) beans, raw	1.6	271
Baked beans, canned	0.5	64
Red kidney beans, raw	1.7	272
Lentils,		
raw	1.0	304
boiled	0.5	99
Peas, split,		
dried	1.3	286
boiled	0.4	103
Chick peas (garbanzos),		
raw	5.7	320
boiled	3.3	144

Nuts

	Fat (g)	Calories
Almonds	53.5	565
Brazil nuts	61.5	619

	Fat (g)	Calories
Chestnuts	2.7	170
Hazelnuts	36.0	380
Coconut, desiccated (shredded)	62.0	604
Peanuts,		
fresh	36.0	351
roasted and salted	49.0	570
Walnuts (English walnuts)	51.5	525

Vegetables (raw, unless otherwise stated)

	Fat (g)	Calories
Asparagus	Tr	18
Aubergine (eggplant)	Tr	14
French beans (fine green beans)	Tr	7
Runner beans (green beans)	0.2	26
Broad beans (fava beans)	0.6	48
Beetroot (beets)	Tr	28
Broccoli tops	Tr	23
Brussel sprouts	Tr	26
Spring cabbage, boiled	Tr	7
Carrots	Tr	23
Cauliflower	Tr	13
Celery	Tr	8
Cucumber	Tr	10
Leeks	Tr	31
Lettuce	0.4	12
Marrow (squash)	Tr	16
Mushrooms	0.6	13
Onions	Tr	23
Parsnips	Tr	49
Peas	0.4	67
Potatoes,	0.4	87
mashed,	5.0	119
roast,	4.8	157
chipped (made into fries)	10.9	253
crisps (chips)	35.9	533
Spinach, boiled	0.5	30

	Fat (g)	Calories
Swede (rutabaga)	Tr	21
Sweetcorn on the cob	2.4	127
Sweetcorn kernels, canned	0.5	76
Tomatoes	Tr	14
Watercress	Tr	14

Fruits

	Fat (g)	Calories
Apples	Tr	46
Apricots,	Tr	28
dried	Tr	182
Avocado	22.2	223
Bananas	0.3	79
Blackberries	Tr	29
Cherries	Tr	47
Blackcurrants	Tr	28
Currants, dried	Tr	243
Dates, dried	Tr	248
Figs, green	Tr	41
Gooseberries	Tr	17
Grapes, black	Tr	61
Grapefruit	Tr	22
Melon	Tr	24
Olives	11.0	103
Oranges	Tr	35
Peaches	Tr	37
Pears	Tr	41
Pineapple, fresh	Tr	46
Plums	Tr	38
Prunes	Tr	161
Raisins	Tr	246
Raspberries	Tr	25
Rhubarb	Tr	6
Strawberries	Tr	26
Sultanas (golden seedless raisins)	Tr	250

	Fat (g)	Calories
Miscellaneous		
Chocolate, milk	30.3	529
Mayonnaise	78.9	718
Ice-cream	6.6	167

Appendix 2

Useful Addresses

Coronary Prevention Group, 102 Gloucester Place, London W1H 3DA

British Heart Foundation, 14 Fitzhardinge Street, London W1H 4DH

Health Education Authority, Hamilton House, Mabledon Place, London WC1H 9TX

Flora Project for Heart Disease Prevention, 24–28 Bloomsbury Way, London WC1A 2PX

Index